THE
Amish
FAMILY
COOKBOOK

JERRY & TINA
EICHER

HARVEST HOUSE PUBLISHERS
EUGENE, OREGON

Cover by Garborg Design Works, Savage, Minnesota
Cover photos © Chris Garborg; Bigstock / mcfields, anyamay

THE AMISH FAMILY COOKBOOK

Copyright © 2012 by Jerry and Tina Eicher

Published by Harvest House Publishers
Eugene, Oregon 97402
www.harvesthousepublishers.com

Library of Congress Cataloging-in-Publication Data
Eicher, Jerry S.
  The Amish family cookbook / Jerry and Tina Eicher.
    p. cm.
  ISBN 978-0-7369-4377-2 (pbk.)
  ISBN 978-0-7369-4378-9 (eBook)
  1. Amish cooking. 2. Cooking, American. I. Eicher, Tina, II. Title
  TX715.E327 2012
  641.5'66--dc23

                                                    2012007742

Printed in China

        12 13 14 15 16 17 18 19 20 / RDS-SK / 10 9 8 7 6 5 4 3   2 1

CONTENTS

A Word from Tina Eicher

Growing up Amish, my mom did a lot of canning and baking. At one point she sold baked goods from our house on Fridays and Saturdays. Breads, cinnamon rolls, pies, and angel food cakes were some of her bestsellers. She would also make noodles, both for sale and for our own use. I remember the spare bed often having noodles drying on it.

The Amish community we moved to when I was eleven also had many good cooks. I still have the community cookbooks they made and use recipes from them.

I cooked infrequently at home as a girl. I would always weasel out of it if I could. Gradually, I got into cooking and found it rewarding when people liked my food. At first, I stayed close to the recipe instructions and amounts. Eventually I realized I could successfully make small changes. But I'm still prone to think I can't make a recipe if I don't have all the ingredients and have to improvise—a thing I'm not nearly as good at as some of the cooks I've watched.

This cookbook has quite a few recipes in the baking sections with chocolate in them. I do not like chocolate or chocolate chips but my family loves them. It's rather handy that way, because I'm not tempted to eat so much.

I am grateful to our daughters, Jolene and Stacie, for all the new bars and cookies they tried (many of them with chocolate) when they went through their baking stages. Their experiments came in very handy when I went to type up the recipes.

I am still surrounded by good cooks. Both of my sisters live in this area and, of course, all the ladies from church. I have also gleaned many good recipes from Jerry's mom, sisters, and sisters-in-law.

I hope you enjoy this cookbook and find many new recipes to try.

God bless!

Tina

APPETIZERS
AND
BEVERAGES

"So what would you do if someone gave you two cows?" the skeptic asked of the three men.

"I'd give both of mine to charity, and expect my reward in heaven," the Quaker said.

"I'd give my two cows to the colony, and they'd keep my family in milk," the Hutterite said.

"I think I'd keep one of my cows, and trade the other for a bull," the Amish man said.

Homestyle Cheesy Garlic Bread

⅔ cup Parmesan cheese
2 sticks (1 cup) butter,
   softened
2 tsp. Worcestershire sauce

½ tsp. pepper
1 tsp. garlic salt
1 loaf French bread, sliced
   (about 1 inch thick)

Mix first five ingredients and spread on both sides of French bread slices. Fry in ungreased nonstick pan until golden brown on both sides.

Note: You can also just make a half batch of the mixture. Cut the French bread in half lengthwise, and spread cut side with mixture. Broil until golden brown. Slice and serve.

A man who waits for a cloudless day to mow his hay may never dry it in time.

Savory Sausage and Rye Bread Bites

1 lb. ground beef
1 lb. ground sausage
1 tsp. oregano
½ tsp. garlic salt
1 lb. Velveeta cheese, cubed
8 oz. pizza sauce

4 oz. canned mushrooms,
   drained and finely
   chopped
2 or more loaves of party rye
   or party sourdough bread

Cook ground beef and sausage until no longer pink; drain. Add oregano, garlic salt, and cheese; stir until cheese is melted. Then add pizza sauce and mushrooms. Lay out the bread slices on cookie sheets. Spread meat mixture on each slice. Place in freezer. When frozen, put them in resealable plastic bags until ready to use.

When ready to use, place on cookie sheets and let them thaw a bit. Broil until lightly browned (5 minutes or so). Watch closely when broiling—they don't take long.

Note: These can also be made without the pizza sauce.

Simple Vegetable Dip

1 package buttermilk Ranch
    salad dressing mix
1 8-oz. package cream cheese,
    softened

16 oz. sour cream

Mix and refrigerate until ready to use.

Don't pull up your garden to see if it's growing.

Easy Party Mix

7 oz. Cheerios
7 oz. Corn Chex
7 oz. Rice Chex (substitute
    Wheat Chex for some of
    the Corn Chex or Rice
    Chex, if desired)
2 cups oil

1 T. Worcestershire sauce
scant 1 tsp. garlic salt
scant 1 tsp. seasoned salt
12 oz. pretzels (substitute
    cheese cracker tidbits, if
    desired)
2 lbs. mixed nuts

In large roaster, mix together the cereals. In another bowl, mix together the oil, Worcestershire sauce, garlic salt, and seasoned salt. Stir this mixture into cereal. Bake at 250° for 1 hour, stirring every 15 minutes. Add the pretzels and nuts. Bake 1 more hour, stirring every 15 minutes. Cool completely before storing in an airtight container. Makes 8 quarts.

Rachel's Fruit Dip

1 8-oz. package cream cheese, softened
¾ cup brown sugar
1 cup sour cream
2 tsp. vanilla
2 tsp. lemon juice
1 cup cold milk
1 3-oz. package instant vanilla pudding mix

Mix in the order given. Chill until ready to serve with fresh fruits.

Appetizer Meatballs or Little Smokies

4 lbs. Italian appetizer-size meatballs, frozen, or Little Smokies
1 32-oz. jar grape jelly
2 12-oz. jars chili sauce
pinch red pepper

Place meatballs in a slow cooker. Mix together remainder of ingredients and pour over meatballs. Cook on high 3 to 4 hours or more, stirring now and then. Turn to low when meatballs are done.

You can also use Little Smokies; same amounts, but less cooking time. Little Smokies are already cooked; they simply need to be heated through before serving.

Blowing at the smoke doesn't help if the chimney is plugged.

Mamm's Eggnog

1 egg, well beaten
2 T. sugar
1 cup half-and-half

¼ tsp. vanilla
nutmeg to taste

Beat together the egg, sugar, and half-and-half. Stir in vanilla and nutmeg to taste.

Thirsty Man's Sweet Lemonade

5 lemons
5 limes
5 oranges

1½–2 cups sugar
3 quarts water

Squeeze the juice from 4 each of the lemons, limes, and oranges. Pour into a gallon container. Add sugar and water. Mix well. Thinly slice the remaining lemon, lime, and orange and add to lemonade as garnish.

Ruth's Dip

2 cans refried beans, mashed
3 or 4 avocados, mashed
2 T. lemon juice
½ tsp. salt
½ tsp. pepper
1–1½ cups sour cream
½ cup mayonnaise

1 package taco seasoning
chopped onion
chopped tomatoes
shredded cheese
sliced ripe olives, if desired
corn or tortilla chips

Spread beans on platter. Mix together the avocados, lemon juice, salt, and pepper. Spread mixture on beans. Mix together the sour cream, mayonnaise, and taco seasoning. Spread on avocado layer. Sprinkle with onion, tomatoes, cheese, and olives, as much of each as you wish. Serve with chips.

The problem with a little sin is that it usually grows into a big one.

Amish Peanut Butter

From *Rebecca's Choice*

Rebecca told herself John's decision was understandable, but the pain wouldn't go away. Her heart ached as she joined in with lunch preparations. She carried peanut butter bowls, refilled the pickle jars, smiled when spoken to, and finally got to eat, the food tasteless in her mouth.

peanut butter
marshmallow crème

maple syrup

Mix together peanut butter, more marshmallow crème than peanut butter, and enough maple syrup to make it easy to spread. Stir and test with table knife to see if you can easily spread it on bread. (You don't want it so thick that the bread tears.)

Serve with bread and butter. Also, pickles, cheese (Colby Jack or Muenster are good choices), and bologna or some kind of meat. (We use deer salami.) I serve all this and soup of some kind. The Amish eat this after church (not the soup).

Note: The secret to this peanut butter is to use more of the marshmallow crème than peanut butter. If you're using store-bought syrup, it takes more than you would think to make it spread easily. This is a big favorite of Jerry's.

Easy Snack Eggs

24 hard-boiled eggs	2 tsp. white vinegar
2 tsp. Dijon mustard	½–1 tsp. salt
2 tsp. prepared mustard	½–1 tsp. pepper
1 cup mayonnaise	paprika
1 cup Miracle Whip	

Bend the branch while it is young.

Cut eggs in half lengthwise and put yolks in a bowl. Mash the yolks. To the yolks add the rest of the ingredients except the paprika and mix thoroughly. Taste to make sure it has enough salt. Fill the egg white halves with yolk mixture and sprinkle with paprika.

I always put in 1 cup of mayonnaise and 1 cup of Miracle Whip. This makes a big batch.

Spinach Cheese Dip

1 8-oz. package cream cheese, softened
1 jar (16 oz.) salsa
1 package (10 oz.) frozen chopped spinach, thawed and squeezed dry
2 cups (8 oz.) shredded Mexican cheese blend, divided
Tortilla chips

In a large bowl, combine the cream cheese, salsa, spinach, and 1 cup cheese blend. Spread into an ungreased 9-inch pie plate. Sprinkle with the remaining cheese. Bake, uncovered, at 350° for 20–25 minutes or until heated through. Serve with tortilla chips.

Avocado Dip

1 medium ripe avocado, halved, seeded, and peeled
4½ tsp. lemon juice
1 small tomato, seeded and finely chopped
¼ cup onion, finely chopped
1 T. green chilies, finely chopped
1 garlic clove, minced
¼ tsp. salt

Mash avocado with lemon juice. Stir in rest of ingredients. Cover and chill. Serve with tortilla chips.

Olive-Onion Cheese Bread

4 cups (16 oz.) shredded
mozzarella cheese
1 cup butter, softened
1 cup mayonnaise
8 green onions, thinly sliced
1 8-oz. can mushroom stems
and pieces, drained and
chopped

1 4½-oz. can chopped ripe
olives
1 loaf unsliced French bread

*Lying in bed
dreaming
never got the
work done.*

Combine the first 6 ingredients. Cut bread in half lengthwise; place on an ungreased baking sheet. Spread with cheese mixture.

Bake at 350° for 15–20 minutes or until cheese is melted. Cut each half into 8 slices.

Honey Oat Clusters

1½ T. vegetable oil
3½ T. honey
1 cup old-fashioned rolled oats
2 T. wheat germ
1½ T. sliced almonds
⅛ tsp. salt

⅛ tsp. cinnamon
⅛ tsp. nutmeg
1½ T. dark or golden raisins
¼ cup butter, cut into small
pieces
¼ cup brown sugar

Preheat oven to 300°. Line a baking sheet with foil.

Mix together oil and 1½ tablespoons honey until well blended. Add oats, wheat germ, almonds, salt, cinnamon, and nutmeg, stirring to coat.

Spread this mixture evenly on baking sheet. Bake, stirring occasionally, until golden in color, about 15 to 20 minutes. Remove from oven. Stir in raisins. Cool for 30 minutes. Transfer granola to a bowl. (Or you can store the granola as is and use it for breakfast cereal.)

Line another baking sheet with waxed paper.

In a small saucepan, bring butter, brown sugar, and remaining honey to a boil over low heat, stirring constantly, until sugar has dissolved and butter and honey have melted, about 5 minutes. Pour butter mixture over granola mixture, tossing with a fork until just combined. Cool slightly.

Using 2 greased teaspoons, shape granola mixture into 1-inch balls. Place balls on prepared baking sheet; flatten slightly. Cool completely.

Icy Holiday Punch

1 6-oz. package cherry gelatin	1 46-oz. can pineapple juice
¾ cup sugar	6 cups cold water
2 cups boiling water	2 liters ginger ale, chilled

Dissolve gelatin and sugar in boiling water. Stir in pineapple juice and cold water. Place in a 4-quart freezer container and freeze overnight. Remove from freezer 2 hours before serving.

Place in a punch bowl. Stir in ginger ale. Yield: 32–36 servings.

Give a man bread and he will eat for a day. Teach him how to plow and he will feed his family for the rest of his life.

Amish Maple Cream Spread

4 cups white sugar
2 pints light or dark corn
   syrup

1 cup water
maple flavoring
2 egg whites

Mix sugar, corn syrup, and water; bring to a boil. Immediately remove from heat. Add maple flavoring to taste. When slightly cooled, beat egg whites until stiff. Beat in syrup.

Ham Cheese Ball

16 oz. cream cheese
8 oz. smoked Cheddar cheese,
   shredded
2 tsp. Worcestershire sauce
1 tsp. garlic salt

½ tsp. seasoned salt
2 packages dried ham,
   chopped fine
2 tsp. parsley flakes
½ cup pecans, finely chopped

With a fork, mix together all ingredients except the parsley and pecans. Refrigerate overnight. Shape into ball and roll in the parsley and pecans until completely covered.

Mini Cherry Cheesecakes

1 cup vanilla wafer crumbs
3 T. butter, melted
1 8-oz. package cream cheese,
    softened
1½ tsp. vanilla
2 tsp. lemon juice

⅓ cup sugar
1 egg

Topping:
1 can cherry pie filling
¼ tsp. almond extract

Combine crumbs and butter. Press gently into bottom of 12 paper-lined muffin cups.

Combine cream cheese, vanilla, lemon juice, sugar, and egg. Beat until smooth. Spoon into crusts. Bake at 375° for 12–15 minutes or until set. Cool.

Mix together the ingredients for the topping and spoon over cheesecakes.

A woman's kisses may fade away, but her good cooking rarely does.

White Sparkling Punch

2 64-oz. containers white
    grape juice

1–2 liters ginger ale

Place grape juice and ginger ale in the refrigerator overnight or until very well chilled. You can place them in the freezer for 1–2 hours before you mix and serve. This will make the punch extra cold and icy.

Mix together white grape juice and ginger ale and serve over ice.

Amish Root Beer

2 cups sugar
¾ tsp. yeast

1 gallon warm water
2 T. root beer extract

Mix together the sugar and yeast. Add other ingredients and mix again. Pour into jug with lid but don't close lid too tightly. Let sit in full sunlight for 4 hours. Chill and serve.

A round wife and a full barn are the signs of good success.

Mocha Punch

1½ quarts water
½ cup instant chocolate drink mix
½ cup sugar
¼ cup instant coffee granules

½ gallon vanilla ice cream
½ gallon chocolate ice cream
1 cup heavy cream, whipped
chocolate curls, optional

In a large saucepan, bring water to a boil. Remove from the heat. Add drink mix, sugar, and coffee; stir until dissolved. Cover and refrigerate for 4 hours or overnight.

About 30 minutes before serving, pour into a punch bowl. Add ice cream by scoopfuls; stir until partially melted. Garnish with dollops of whipped cream and chocolate curls if desired. Yield: 20–25 servings (about 5 quarts).

Sensational Slush

½ cup sugar
1 3-oz. package strawberry
    gelatin
2 cups boiling water
2 cups sliced fresh
    strawberries
1 cup unsweetened pineapple
    juice

1 12-oz. can frozen lemonade
    concentrate, thawed
1 12-oz. can frozen limeade
    concentrate, thawed
2 cups cold water
2 liters lemon-lime soda,
    chilled

In a large bowl, dissolve sugar and gelatin in boiling water.
Place the strawberries and pineapple juice in a blender or food
processor; cover and process until smooth. Add to the gelatin
mixture. Stir in lemonade, limeade, and cold water. Cover and
freeze for 8 hours or overnight.

Remove from the freezer 45 minutes before serving. For each
serving, combine ½ cup slush mixture with ½ cup lemon-lime
soda; stir well. Yield: 20 servings.

Orange Sherbet Punch

4 cups water, divided
2 3-oz. packages strawberry
    gelatin
1½ cups sugar
1 46-oz. can pineapple juice

1 46-oz. can orange juice
1 cup lemon juice
½ gallon orange sherbet,
    softened
1 liter ginger ale, chilled

Heat 2 cups water to boiling; add gelatin and sugar, stirring until
dissolved. Add 2 cups cold water and fruit juices. Chill until
ready to serve. Just before serving, spoon in sherbet and pour in
ginger ale. Yield: 6½ quarts.

Spiced Cider

2 quarts apple cider
½ cup brown sugar
3 cinnamon sticks (3 inches)

½–1 tsp. ground allspice
⅛ tsp. salt
⅛ tsp. nutmeg

In a large saucepan, combine all ingredients; bring to a boil. Reduce heat; cover and simmer for 20 minutes. Discard cinnamon sticks. Use additional cinnamon sticks for stirrers if desired.

Yield: 8–10 servings (about 2 quarts).

If you want to keep a secret, don't whisper in your wife's ear.

BREAKFAST

Breakfast Cereal

10 cups quick oatmeal
¾–1 cup brown sugar
2 cups flaked coconut
2 packages (not boxes)
  graham crackers,
  crushed

2 tsp. baking soda
1 cup chopped pecans or
  walnuts
1 tsp. salt
1 cup butter, melted
1 cup butterscotch chips

Mix together all ingredients except butterscotch chips. Spread on cookie sheet. Bake at 300° for 40 minutes, stirring every 10 minutes. Remove from oven and add butterscotch chips. Stir several times while cooling.

Sausage and Egg Casserole

1 lb. sausage, mild
6 eggs
2 cups milk
1 tsp. salt

1 tsp. dry mustard
2 slices white bread, cubed
1 cup grated cheese

Brown and drain sausage. In a large mixing bowl, beat the eggs. Add the milk, salt, and dry mustard. Stir in bread, cheese, and sausage. Pour into a greased 12 x 8-inch pan and refrigerate overnight. Bake at 350° for 45 minutes. Let stand a few minutes before serving.

When a person slaps you on the back, he may be trying to help you swallow something.

Blueberry Sour Cream Pancakes

2 cups flour
¼ cup sugar
4 tsp. baking powder
½ tsp. salt
2 eggs

1½ cups milk
1 cup sour cream
⅓ cup butter, melted
1 cup fresh or frozen
    blueberries

Combine flour, sugar, baking powder, and salt. In another bowl, beat eggs. Add milk, sour cream, and butter. Stir into dry ingredients just until blended. Fold in blueberries. Pour batter by ¼-cupfuls onto a greased hot griddle. Turn when bubbles form on top of pancakes. Remove from pan when second side is golden brown. Yield: about 20 pancakes.

Blueberry French Toast

12 slices day-old white bread,
    crusts removed
2 8-oz. packages cream cheese
1 cup fresh blueberries
12 eggs
2 cups milk
⅓ cup maple syrup

Sauce:
1 cup sugar
2 T. corn starch
1 cup water
1 cup fresh blueberries
1 T. butter
½ tsp. lemon juice (optional)

Cut bread into 1-inch cubes; place half in a greased 9 x 13-inch pan. Cut cream cheese into 1-inch cubes; place over bread. Top with blueberries and remaining bread. Beat eggs. Add milk and maple syrup; mix well. Pour over bread mixture. Cover and refrigerate overnight. Remove from refrigerator 30 minutes before baking. Cover and bake at 350° for 30 minutes. Uncover and bake for another 25 to 30 minutes or until golden brown and center is set.

To make the sauce: In a saucepan, combine sugar and cornstarch; add water. Bring to a boil, stirring constantly. Boil for 3 minutes, continuing to stir constantly. Stir in blueberries. Simmer for 8 to 10 minutes or until berries have burst. Stir in lemon juice and butter. Serve over French toast.

Note: I usually make a double batch of the sauce. Some people prefer maple syrup instead of the sauce.

Bacon, Egg, and Cheese Bagel

2 or 3 slices bacon, fried	1 bagel (we like Nature's Own Original Bagels)
1 egg, fried, yolk hard	1 slice American or Cheddar cheese
mayonnaise or soft butter	

I fry a pack of bacon at a time and freeze it until needed, so these breakfast bagels are quick to make.

While egg is frying, toast bagel in toaster. Spread mayonnaise or butter on a bagel half. Then layer egg, cheese, 2 or 3 slices of bacon (heated in microwave if previously cooked and refrigerated), and top with the other half of bagel, which has also been spread with mayonnaise or butter.

Our son Christopher came up with these, inspired by the McDonald's Bacon, Egg & Cheese Bagel.

Death isn't the greatest loss in life. It's what dies inside of us while we live.

Cheese and Bacon Frittata

6 eggs
1 cup milk
1 green onion or a bit of
    onion, minced
2 T. butter, melted
½ tsp. salt

⅛ tsp. pepper
1 cup shredded Cheddar
    cheese
6 slices bacon, fried and
    crumbled

Beat eggs, milk, onion, butter, salt, and pepper until well blended. Pour into greased 9-inch square pan. Sprinkle with cheese and bacon. Bake at 400° for 20 minutes.

Note: I make a double batch and put it in a 9 x 13-inch pan and bake it at 375° for about 40 minutes.

*If you
want to
make your
money last,
you have
to make
it first.*

Great Granola

2 cups old-fashioned oats
½ cup chopped almonds
½ cup salted pumpkin seeds
    or pepitas
½ cup chopped walnuts
¼ cup chopped pecans
¼ cup sesame seeds
¼ cup sunflower kernels

⅓ cup honey
¼ cup brown sugar
¼ cup maple syrup
2 T. toasted wheat germ
2 T. canola oil
1 tsp. ground cinnamon
1 tsp. vanilla extract
1 7-oz. package dried fruit bits

In a large bowl, combine the oats, almonds, pumpkin seeds, walnuts, pecans, sesame seeds, and sunflower kernels; set aside. In a small saucepan, combine the honey, brown sugar, maple syrup, wheat germ, canola oil, and cinnamon. Cook and stir over medium heat for 4–5 minutes or until smooth. Remove from heat; stir in vanilla. Pour over oat mixture and toss to coat.

Transfer to a greased cookie sheet. Bake at 350° for 22–27 minutes or until golden brown, stirring occasionally. Cool completely. Stir in fruit bits. Store in airtight container.

Note: If your granola is still sticky instead of crispy when cooled, put it back in the oven and bake an additional 5 or 10 minutes. My family is not crazy about the fruit bits so I sometimes omit them. I left out the wheat germ one time and it was very good anyway.

Breakfast Pizza

1 8-oz. tube crescent rolls
4 eggs
½ cup milk
¼ tsp. each, salt and
    pepper
1 T. butter, melted
¼ cup onions (optional)

1 cup chopped bacon, ham, or
    sausage
4 oz. mozzarella cheese or
    cheese of your choice,
    grated (approximately
    1 cup)
1 T. chives, chopped

Press crescent roll dough into 13 x 9-inch cake pan. Beat the eggs and then add the rest of the ingredients. Pour on top of dough and bake at 350° for 30 minutes.

Old-Time Cake Donuts

2 T. unsalted butter, softened	3 tsp. cinnamon, divided
1½ cups sugar, divided	½ tsp. salt
3 eggs	⅛ tsp. nutmeg
4 cups flour	¾ cup 2% milk
1 T. baking powder	Oil for deep-fat frying

In a large bowl, beat butter and 1 cup sugar until crumbly, about 2 minutes. Add eggs, one at a time, beating well after each addition. Combine the flour, baking powder, 1 tsp. cinnamon, salt, and nutmeg; add to butter mixture, alternately with milk, beating well after each addition. Cover and refrigerate for 2 hours.

Turn onto heavily floured surface; pat dough to ¼-inch thickness. Cut with a floured 2½-inch doughnut cutter. In an electric skillet or deep fryer, heat oil to 375°. Fry donuts, a few at a time, until golden brown on both sides. Drain on paper towels. Combine remaining sugar and cinnamon; roll warm donuts in mixture.

Being human is a privilege, not an excuse.

Baked Apple French Toast

20 slices French bread (1 inch thick)	½ tsp. nutmeg
1 21-oz. can apple pie filling	***Topping:***
8 eggs	1 cup brown sugar
2 cups milk	½ cup cold butter, cubed
2 tsp. vanilla	1 cup chopped pecans
½ tsp. cinnamon	2 T. corn syrup

Arrange 10 slices of bread in a greased 13 x 9-inch baking dish. Spread with pie filling; top with remaining bread. Combine eggs, milk, vanilla, cinnamon, and nutmeg. Pour over bread. Cover and refrigerate overnight. Remove from refrigerator 30 minutes before baking.

In the morning, place brown sugar in small bowl. Cut in butter until mixture resembles coarse crumbs. Stir in pecans and corn syrup. Sprinkle over French toast. Bake uncovered at 350° for 35–40 minutes or until knife inserted near the center comes out clean.

Blueberry Cheesecake Flapjacks

1 3-oz. package cream cheese, softened
¾ cup whipped topping
1 cup flour
½ cup graham cracker crumbs
1 T. sugar
1 tsp. baking powder
½ tsp. baking soda
¼ tsp. salt
2 eggs, lightly beaten
1¼ cups buttermilk
¼ cup butter, melted
1 cup fresh or frozen blueberries
¾ cup maple syrup, warmed

For topping, beat cream cheese and whipped topping until smooth. Chill until ready to serve. In a large bowl, combine flour, graham cracker crumbs, sugar, baking powder, baking soda, and salt. In another bowl, combine eggs, buttermilk, and melted butter; add to dry ingredients just until moistened. Fold in blueberries. Pour batter by ¼ cupfuls onto a greased hot griddle; turn when bubbles form on top. Cook until second side is golden brown. Spread topping over pancakes. Top with warm syrup; sprinkle with additional blueberries if desired.

If you must doubt, doubt your doubts, not your beliefs.

Baked Oatmeal

3 cups quick-cooking oats
1 cup brown sugar
2 tsp. baking powder
1 tsp. salt

1 tsp. cinnamon
2 eggs
1 cup milk
½ cup butter, melted

Combine the dry ingredients. Whisk together the wet ingredients and add to dry ingredients. Pour into a greased 9-inch square pan. Bake at 350° for 40 to 50 minutes. Serve warm with milk.

Baked Blueberry and Peach Oatmeal

3 cups old-fashioned oats
½ cup brown sugar
2 tsp. baking powder
½ tsp. salt
2 egg whites
1 egg
1¼ cups fat-free milk

¼ cup canola oil
1 tsp. vanilla
1 15-oz. can sliced peaches, drained and chopped
1 cup fresh or frozen blueberries
⅓ cup chopped walnuts

In a large bowl, combine the oats, brown sugar, baking powder, and salt. In another bowl, whisk together the egg whites, egg, milk, canola oil, and vanilla; stir into dry ingredients. Let stand for 5 minutes. Stir in peaches and blueberries and pour the batter into an 11 x 7-inch baking dish coated with cooking spray. Sprinkle with walnuts. Bake uncovered at 350° for 35 to 40 minutes. Note: This is a healthier version of baked oatmeal.

Maple Bran Cereal

16 cups (4 lbs.) whole wheat
  flour
4½ cups (2 lbs.) brown sugar
2 tsp. salt
1 T. baking soda

5 cups buttermilk
1½ sticks butter, melted
1 T. vanilla
1 T. maple flavoring

Mix together the flour, brown sugar, and salt. In another bowl, combine the baking soda with the buttermilk. Mix buttermilk mixture with dry ingredient mixture. Add butter and flavorings. Bake in two greased 13 x 9-inch pans at 350° for 45 minutes to 1 hour or until a toothpick comes out clean. Cool. Cut into chunks and grate. (I use a screen my dad made for my mom for this purpose. The holes in it are about 1 centimeter square.) Put in a large roaster and toast at 250° for 2 hours or so, until crisp, stirring often. Cool, stirring now and then. Store in airtight container.

The hardest mountains in the world to climb are the ones made out of molehills.

Creamed Eggs

½ cup butter
½ cup flour
1 quart milk
salt and pepper, to taste
5–6 hard-boiled eggs,
  chopped

½ cup or more of grated
  Cheddar cheese
fried bacon, fried sausage, or
  chopped ham

Melt butter; add flour. Gradually add milk, stirring constantly until thickened and bubbly. Add salt and pepper to taste. Add eggs, cheese, and meat of choice. Stir till heated through and cheese is melted. Serve over toast. Very good!

Breakfast Burritos

1 16-oz. bag frozen Southern-
style hash browns
12 eggs
1 large onion, chopped
1 green pepper, chopped
½ lb. bulk pork sausage,
thoroughly cooked and
drained

12 10-inch flour tortillas,
warmed
3 cups (12 oz.) shredded
Cheddar cheese
salsa, optional

*They that
know God
will be
humble,
and they
that know
themselves
cannot be
proud.*

Fry hash browns according to package directions; remove and set aside. Beat eggs; add onions and pepper. Pour into the same skillet; cook and stir until eggs are set. Remove from heat. Add hash browns and sausage; mix gently. Place about ¾ cup of the filling on each tortilla and top with about ¼ cup cheese. Roll up and place on a greased baking sheet. Bake at 350° for 15–20 minutes or until heated through and cheese is melted. Serve with salsa if desired.

Hash Brown Quiche

3 cups frozen loose-packed
shredded hash browns,
thawed
⅓ cup butter, melted
1 cup fully cooked ham, diced
1 cup (4 oz.) shredded
Cheddar cheese

¼ cup green pepper, diced
2 eggs
½ cup milk
½ tsp. salt
¼ tsp. pepper

Press hash browns between paper towels to remove excess moisture. Press into the bottom and up the sides of an ungreased 9-inch pie plate. Drizzle with butter. Bake at 425° for 25 minutes. Remove from oven and reduce temperature to 350°.

Combine the ham, cheese, and green pepper; spoon over crust. Beat eggs, milk, salt, and pepper. Pour over all. Bake at 350° for 25–30 minutes or until knife inserted in center comes out clean. Allow to stand for 10 minutes before cutting. Yield: 6 servings.

Basic Omelet and Farmer's Omelet

Mix 3 eggs with fork just until whites and yolks are blended. Heat 1 tablespoon butter in 8-inch skillet over medium-high heat. As butter melts, tilt skillet in all directions to coat sides and bottom of skillet thoroughly. When butter just begins to brown, skillet is hot enough to use.

Quickly pour eggs all at once into skillet. Start sliding skillet back and forth rapidly over heat. At the same time, stir quickly with fork to spread eggs continuously over bottom of skillet as they thicken. Let stand over heat a few seconds to lightly brown bottom of omelet. Do not overcook—omelet will continue to cook after folding. Tilt skillet; run fork under edge of omelet, then jerk skillet sharply to loosen eggs from bottom of skillet. Fold portion of omelet nearest you just to center. Flip onto warm plate.

To make a Farmer's Omelet: There are so many things you can add to the omelet before folding: bacon, cheese, chopped ham, chopped onion or green onion, and chopped green pepper are a few ideas. You can add more eggs for a bigger omelet, and topping an omelet with salsa is good. Omelets can also be a quick supper.

We make a living by what we get, but we make a life by what we give.

Cornmeal Mush with Maple Syrup

¾ cup cornmeal
¾ cup cold water
2½ cups boiling water
¾ tsp. salt

2 T. butter
flour
maple syrup

Mix cornmeal and cold water in saucepan. Stir in boiling water and salt. Cook, stirring constantly, until mixture thickens and boils; reduce heat. Cover and simmer 10 minutes. Spread in greased loaf pan. Cover and refrigerate until firm, at least 12 hours.

Cut loaf into ½-inch slices or less. Heat butter in skillet until melted. Coat slices with flour; cook in butter until brown on both sides. Serve hot with maple syrup or molasses.

Overnight Breakfast Bars

1¼ cups flour
1½ cups old-fashioned oats
2 T. flax meal, optional
1 tsp. baking powder
1 T. baking soda
¼ tsp. salt
2 tsp. cinnamon
1 cup sugar
½ cup brown sugar
⅔ cup butter, softened

2 eggs
1⅓ cups buttermilk or plain yogurt
2 medium apples, peeled, cored, and chopped

Topping:
1 cup chopped walnuts or pecans
½ cup brown sugar
1 tsp. cinnamon

Combine flour, oats, flax meal, baking powder, soda, salt, and cinnamon; set aside. Combine sugars and butter; beat well.

Blend in eggs and buttermilk. Put mixer on low and gradually add flour mixture, beating just until blended. Fold in apples. Pour into a greased 13 x 9-inch pan. For topping, combine walnuts, brown sugar, and cinnamon. Sprinkle evenly over batter. Cover and refrigerate overnight. Preheat oven to 350°. Uncover pan and let stand for 30 minutes. Bake 45 minutes, or until toothpick comes out clean.

Rebecca's Oatmeal Pancake Mix

From *Rebecca's Promise*

Rebecca poked her head into the kitchen.
"Pancakes?" she asked, seeing her mother mixing batter.
"Yes," Mattie smiled. "When I saw it was snowing, I decided this was the morning for pancakes. Lester will take the time to eat properly because he can't get outside work done."

4 cups old-fashioned oats
2 cups flour
2 cups whole wheat flour
1 cup brown sugar
1 cup instant nonfat dry milk
3 T. baking powder
2 T. cinnamon, optional

5 tsp. salt
½ tsp. cream of tartar

For Pancakes:

2 eggs
⅓ cup canola oil
2 cups pancake mix
1 cup water

For mix, combine all ingredients well. Store in a sealed container. Makes 10 cups.

For pancakes, beat eggs; gradually beat in oil. Alternately add pancake mix and water; blend well. If batter seems too thick, you can add a bit more water. Fry as you would any pancakes.

There's a difference between good sound reasons and reasons that sound good.

Peanut Butter Granola

18 cups oatmeal
3 cups coconut
1½ cups sunflower seeds
1½ cups slivered almonds
1½ cups pecans, chopped
1 cup butter
½ cup vegetable oil

½ cup peanut butter
½ cup honey
1 cup maple syrup or 1½ cups
  brown sugar
1 T. vanilla
1 T. water
1 tsp. salt

Mix oatmeal, coconut, sunflower seeds, almonds, and pecans.
Mix all other ingredients and heat. Pour syrup over dry
ingredients to coat everything. Let set for 2 hours. Press into two
13 x 9-inch pans. Bake at 250° for 30 minutes. Stir well. Store in
airtight containers.

Maple Granola

12 cups rolled oats
2 cups coconut
1 cup slivered almonds
1 cup chopped pecans
1 cup chopped walnuts
2 tsp. salt
¾ cup olive oil
1 cup honey
2 tsp. vanilla

2 tsp. maple flavoring
¼ cup raw cashew pieces
½ cup chopped dates
¼ cup raw chopped Brazil
  nuts
¾ cup raisins
¾ cup sunflower seeds
¼ cup flaxseed

Stir together the oats, coconut, almonds, pecans, walnuts, and
salt. Combine oil, honey, vanilla, and maple flavoring. Add to
oats mixture and stir. Pour into two 13 x 9-inch pans and bake at
275° for approximately 1½ hours. Let cool before stirring if you
prefer chunks. Add remaining ingredients to cooled granola.

Maple French Toast Bake

12 slices bread, cubed	8 eggs
1 8-oz. package cream cheese, cubed	1 cup milk
	½ cup maple syrup

Arrange half of the bread in a greased shallow 2-quart baking dish. Top with the cream cheese and remaining bread. In a bowl, whisk together the eggs, milk, and syrup; pour over bread. Cover and refrigerate overnight. Remove from the refrigerator 30 minutes before baking. Cover and bake at 350° for 30 minutes. Uncover; bake 20–25 minutes longer or until golden brown. Serve with additional syrup.

The way some people look for faults, you'd think there's a reward.

CAKES

White Texas Sheet Cake

1 cup butter
1 cup water
2 cups flour
1 tsp. salt
2 cups sugar
1 tsp. baking powder
¼ tsp. baking soda
2 eggs, beaten

1 tsp. almond extract
½ cup sour cream

Icing:
½ cup butter
¼ cup milk
4½ cups powdered sugar
½ tsp. almond extract
1 cup chopped walnuts

Bring water and butter to a boil. Remove from heat and stir in the rest of the ingredients for cake. Pour into greased cookie sheet and bake at 375° for 20–22 minutes or until cake is golden brown and toothpick inserted near the center comes out clean. Let cool for 20 minutes. For icing, bring milk and butter to a boil. Remove from heat and stir in powdered sugar and almond extract. Add walnuts. Spread over warm cake.

Difficulty is a miracle in its first stage.

Pineapple Cake

2 cups flour
2 cups sugar
2 tsp. baking soda
2 eggs
1 20-oz. can crushed
   pineapple

Frosting:
½ cup butter, softened
1 8-oz. package cream cheese,
   softened
2 cups powdered sugar
1 tsp. vanilla

Mix first five ingredients. Pour into greased 13 x 9-inch pan and bake at 350° for 45 minutes. For frosting, cream together butter and cream cheese. Add powdered sugar and vanilla and beat until smooth. Frost cake immediately while still hot.

Blueberry Buckle

¾ cup sugar
¼ cup shortening
1 egg
2 tsp. baking powder
½ tsp. salt
2 cups flour
½ cup milk

2 cups fresh blueberries
Crumbs:
½ cup sugar
⅓ cup flour
½ tsp. ground cinnamon
¼ cup softened butter

Cream together sugar and shortening. Mix in egg. In another bowl, mix together the dry ingredients. Add flour mixture alternately with milk. Toss blueberries with a bit of flour and add to batter. Spread into greased 8 x 8-inch pan.

For crumbs, combine sugar, flour, and cinnamon. Cut in butter. Sprinkle over batter. Bake at 375° for 25–30 minutes.

Creamy Chocolate Cupcakes

1½ cups flour
1 tsp. baking soda
1 cup sugar
½ tsp. salt
¼ cup baking cocoa
2 eggs
1 T. white vinegar
¾ cup water
1 tsp. vanilla extract
⅓ cup vegetable oil

Filling:
⅓ cup sugar
1 8-oz. package cream cheese, softened
1 egg, lightly beaten
⅛ tsp. salt
1 cup (6 oz.) semisweet chocolate chips
Topping:
1 cup chopped walnuts

For cupcakes, mix together the dry ingredients. Add the rest of the cupcake ingredients and mix well. Pour batter into 18 greased or paper-lined muffin cups.

For filling, beat sugar and cream cheese together; add egg and salt and mix well. Fold in chocolate chips. Drop by tablespoonfuls into center of each cupcake. Sprinkle with walnuts. Bake at 350° for 25–30 minutes or until toothpick inserted near center comes out clean.

Red Velvet Cake

½ cup butter, softened

1½ cups sugar

2 eggs

2 bottles (1 oz. each) red food coloring

1 T. white vinegar

1 tsp. vanilla extract

2¼ cups cake flour

2 T. baking cocoa

1 tsp. baking soda

1 tsp. salt

1 cup buttermilk

Frosting:

1 T. cornstarch

½ cup water

2 cups butter, softened

2 tsp. vanilla extract

3½ cups powdered sugar

Anyone who practices what he preaches doesn't have to preach much.

In a large bowl, cream together the butter and sugar until light and fluffy. Add eggs, one at a time, beating well after each one. Beat in the food coloring, vinegar, and vanilla. Combine the flour, cocoa, baking soda, and salt; add to creamed mixture alternately with buttermilk, beating well after each addition. Pour into two greased and floured 9-inch round baking pans. Bake at 350° for 20–25 minutes or until a toothpick inserted near the center comes out clean. Cool for 10 minutes before removing from pans to wire racks to cool completely.

For frosting: In a small saucepan, combine cornstarch and water until smooth. Cook and stir over medium heat for 2–3 minutes or until thickened and opaque. Cool to room temperature.

In a large bowl, beat butter and vanilla until light and fluffy. Beat in cornstarch mixture. Gradually add powdered sugar; beat until frosting is light and fluffy. Spread frosting between layers and over top and sides of cake.

Amish Upside-Down Berry Cake

½ cup chopped walnuts
1 cup fresh or frozen
    blueberries
1 cup fresh or frozen
    raspberries, halved
1 cup sliced fresh strawberries
¼ cup sugar
1 3-oz. package raspberry
    gelatin

1 box yellow cake mix
2 eggs
1¼ cups water
2 T. canola oil
1½ cups miniature
    marshmallows

In a well-greased 13 x 9-inch baking pan, layer walnuts and berries; sprinkle with sugar and gelatin. In a large bowl, combine the cake mix, eggs, water, and oil; beat on low speed for 30 seconds. Beat on medium speed for 2 minutes. Fold in marshmallows. Pour over top. Bake at 350° for 35–40 minutes or until toothpick inserted near center comes out clean. Cool for 5 minutes before inverting onto a serving platter.

Cream Puff Cake

1 cup water
½ cup butter, cubed
1 cup flour
4 eggs

Filling:
1 8-oz. package cream cheese,
    softened

2½ cups milk
3 packages (3.3 oz. each)
    instant white chocolate or
    vanilla pudding mix
1 8-oz. carton frozen whipped
    topping, thawed

In a large saucepan, bring water and butter to a boil. Add flour all at once and stir until a smooth ball forms. Remove from heat; let stand for 5 minutes. Add the eggs, one at a time, beating well after each addition. Continue beating until smooth and shiny. Transfer to a greased 13 x 9-inch baking dish. Bake at 400° for 22–26 minutes or until puffed and golden brown. Cool completely.

For filling, beat the cream cheese, milk, and pudding mixes until smooth. Spread over the crust; refrigerate for 20 minutes. Spread with whipped topping. Chill until ready to serve.

Banana Cupcakes with Lemon Butter Frosting

Some people work hard to keep their children from having the problems which made men out of their fathers and women out of their mothers.

½ cup shortening
1½ cups sugar
2 eggs
1 cup mashed ripe bananas
1 tsp. vanilla extract
2 cups flour
¾ tsp. baking soda
½ tsp. baking powder

½ tsp. salt
½ cup buttermilk

Lemon Butter Frosting:
2 cups powdered sugar
⅓ cup butter, softened
3 T. mashed ripe bananas
1 T. lemon juice

Cream together the shortening and sugar until light and fluffy. Add eggs, one at a time, beating well after each addition. Beat in bananas and vanilla. Combine the flour, baking soda, baking powder, and salt; add to creamed mixture alternately with buttermilk, beating well after each addition. Fill paper-lined muffin cups two-thirds full. Bake at 375° for 18–22 minutes or until toothpick comes out clean. Cool for 10 minutes before removing from pan. Cool completely. Combine the frosting ingredients; beat until light and fluffy. Frost cupcakes.

Apple Cream Cheese Bundt Cake

Cream Cheese Filling:
1 8-oz. package cream cheese, softened
¼ cup butter, softened
½ cup sugar
1 large egg
2 T. flour
1 tsp. vanilla extract

Apple Cake Batter:
1 cup pecans, finely chopped
3 cups flour
1 cup sugar
1 cup brown sugar
2 tsp. cinnamon
1 tsp. salt

1 tsp. baking soda
1 tsp. nutmeg
½ tsp. allspice
3 large eggs, lightly beaten
¾ cup canola oil
¾ cup applesauce
1 tsp. vanilla extract
3 cups Gala apples, peeled and finely chopped

Praline Frosting:
½ cup brown sugar
¼ cup butter
3 T. milk
1 tsp. vanilla extract
1 cup powdered sugar

Life is as uncertain as a grapefruit's squirt.

Prepare filling: Beat first 3 ingredients at medium speed until blended and smooth. Add egg, flour, and vanilla; beat just until blended.

Prepare batter: Preheat oven to 350°. Bake pecans in a shallow pan 8–10 minutes or until toasted and fragrant, stirring halfway through. Stir together flour and next 7 ingredients; stir in eggs and next 3 ingredients, stirring just until dry ingredients are moistened. Stir in apples and pecans.

Spoon two-thirds of batter into a greased and floured 14-cup Bundt pan. Spoon on the Cream Cheese Filling, leaving a 1-inch border around edges of pan. Swirl filling through cake batter using a paring knife. Spoon remaining batter over Cream Cheese Filling. Bake for 1–1¼ hours or until a long wooden pick inserted in center comes out clean. Cool cake in pan on a wire rack 15 minutes; remove from pan to wire rack and cool completely (about 2 hours).

Prepare frosting: Bring brown sugar, butter, and milk to a boil, whisking constantly. Boil 1 minute, whisking constantly. Remove from heat; stir in vanilla. Gradually whisk in powdered sugar until smooth; stir gently 3–5 minutes or until mixture begins to cool and thickens slightly. Pour immediately over cooled cake.

Buttermilk Cake with Caramel Icing

1 cup butter, softened
2⅓ cups sugar
3 eggs
1½ tsp. vanilla extract
3 cups flour
1 tsp. baking powder
½ tsp. baking soda
1 cup buttermilk

Icing:
¼ cup butter, cubed
½ cup brown sugar
⅓ cup heavy whipping cream
1 cup powdered sugar

Every man must live with the man he makes of himself.

Cream together the butter and sugar until light and fluffy. Add eggs, one at a time, beating well after each addition. Beat in vanilla. Combine flour, baking powder, and baking soda; add to creamed mixture alternately with buttermilk, beating well after each addition (batter will be thick). Pour into greased and floured 10-inch fluted tube pan. Bake at 350° for 45–50 minutes or until a toothpick comes out clean. Cool for 10 minutes before removing from pan. Cool completely.

For icing: In a small saucepan, combine butter, brown sugar, and cream. Bring to a boil over medium heat, stirring constantly. Remove from the heat; cool for 5–10 minutes. Gradually beat in powdered sugar until smooth. Drizzle over cake.

Caramel Chocolate Cake

1 dark chocolate cake mix

1 can sweetened condensed milk

11 oz. caramel ice cream topping

16 oz. whipped topping

Heath bits or English toffee bits

Bake cake according to package directions. As soon as cake is finished baking, poke holes in it with a wooden spoon handle. Pour sweetened condensed milk over it right away and then the caramel. Let cool. Top with whipped topping and sprinkle liberally with toffee bits. Refrigerate.

Usually the less we know the longer it takes to explain.

Angel Food Cake

1 cup flour

1 T. cornstarch

1 tsp. baking powder

1½ cups powdered sugar

1¾ cups egg whites, room temperature

1½ tsp. cream of tartar

¼ tsp. salt

1 cup sugar

1½ tsp. vanilla

½ tsp. almond flavoring

Sift together flour, cornstarch, baking powder, and powdered sugar 3 times. In a large bowl, beat egg whites till foamy; add cream of tartar and salt. Gradually add sugar and beat until stiff. Fold in vanilla and almond flavoring. Sift in flour mixture gradually, folding it in. Pour into a tube pan and run a knife through the batter. Bake at 350° for 35–40 minutes. Turn upside down and cool completely before serving.

Note: You may use cake flour instead of the first three ingredients. This was my mom's recipe. Her angel food cakes were amazing.

Cinnamon Coffee Cake

1 cup butter, softened
2¾ cups sugar, divided
2 tsp. vanilla
4 eggs
3 cups flour
2 tsp. baking powder

1 tsp. baking soda
1 tsp. salt
2 cups (16 oz.) sour cream
2 T. cinnamon
½ cup chopped walnuts

Cream together butter and 2 cups sugar until fluffy. Add the vanilla. Add the eggs, one at a time, beating well after each addition. Combine flour, baking powder, baking soda, and salt; add alternately with sour cream, beating just enough after each addition to keep batter smooth. Spoon one-third of the batter into a greased 10-inch tube pan. Combine the cinnamon, nuts, and remaining sugar; sprinkle one-third over batter in pan. Repeat layers two more times. Bake at 350° for 70 minutes or until cake tests done. Cool for 10 minutes. Remove from pan and cool completely. Yield: 10–16 servings.

A great favorite.

Moist Chocolate Cake

2 cups flour
1 tsp. salt
1 tsp. baking powder
2 tsp. baking soda
¾ cup baking cocoa
2 cups sugar
1 cup vegetable oil
1 cup hot brewed coffee
1 cup milk
2 eggs

1 tsp. vanilla

Icing:
1 cup milk
5 T. flour
½ cup butter, softened
½ cup shortening
1 cup sugar
1 tsp. vanilla

Sift together all dry ingredients. Add oil, coffee, and milk; mix at medium speed for 2 minutes. Add eggs and vanilla; beat 2 minutes more. Pour into two greased and floured 9-inch cake pans (or two 8-inch cake pans and six muffin cups). Bake at 325° for 25–30 minutes.

Meanwhile, for icing, combine the milk and flour in a saucepan; cook until thick. Cover and refrigerate. Beat together the butter, shortening, sugar, and vanilla until creamy. Add chilled milk/flour mixture and beat for 10 minutes. Frost cooled cake. Yield: 12 servings.

We don't realize how wonderful today is until tomorrow.

Saucy Apple Cake

1 cup sugar
¼ cup shortening
1 egg, lightly beaten
1 cup flour
1 tsp. baking soda
½ tsp. cinnamon
¼ tsp. salt
2 cups peeled and shredded
    tart apples
¼ cup chopped walnuts

Vanilla Sauce:
1 cup sugar
2 T. cornstarch
½ cup half-and-half
½ cup butter
1½ tsp. vanilla

In a mixing bowl, cream sugar and shortening. Add egg and mix well. Add dry ingredients; mix well. Fold in the apples and walnuts. Spread in a greased 8-inch square baking pan. Bake at 350° for 35–40 minutes or until a toothpick comes out clean. For sauce, combine sugar, cornstarch, and cream in a saucepan. Bring to a boil over medium heat; boil for 2 minutes. Remove from heat. Add butter and vanilla; stir until butter is melted. Serve warm over warm cake. Yield: 9 servings.

Honey Bun Cake

1 box Betty Crocker Super
    Moist butter yellow cake
    mix
2 sticks butter, softened
4 eggs
8 oz. sour cream

½ cup brown sugar
⅓ cup chopped pecans
2 tsp. cinnamon
2 cups powdered sugar
2 T. milk
2 tsp. vanilla

Heat oven to 350°. Grease bottom only of 13 x 9-inch pan. Remove ½ cup dry cake mix; reserve. Beat remaining dry cake mix, butter, eggs, and sour cream on medium speed 2 minutes. Spread half of the batter in pan. Stir together reserved dry cake mix, brown sugar, pecans, and cinnamon; sprinkle over batter in pan. Carefully spread remaining batter evenly over pecan mixture. Bake 40–45 minutes.

Meanwhile mix last 3 ingredients, adding additional milk if necessary. Poke top of warm cake with fork then pour glaze over it. Cool completely.

Zucchini Cake

2 cups sugar
1 cup oil
3 eggs
1 tsp. vanilla
2 cups flour
1 tsp. cinnamon
1 tsp. salt
2 tsp. baking soda
¼ tsp. baking powder
2 cups shredded zucchini
¾ cup quick-cooking oats

1 cup chopped nuts
½ cup coconut

Frosting:
3 oz. softened cream cheese
½ cup softened butter
2½ cups powdered sugar
2 tsp. vanilla

Stir together sugar and oil. Beat in eggs and vanilla, then stir in flour, cinnamon, salt, baking soda, and baking powder until combined. Fold in zucchini, oats, nuts, and coconut with a rubber spatula. Pour into greased 13 x 9-inch pan. Bake at 350° for 30–35 minutes. Cool.

For frosting, cream together the cream cheese and butter. Mix in powdered sugar and vanilla. Spread on cake.

Coconut Layer Cake

5 eggs, separated
½ cup butter, softened
½ cup shortening
2 cups sugar
1 tsp. vanilla
2 cups flour
½ tsp. baking soda
1 cup buttermilk
2 cups flaked coconut
½ cup chopped pecans, optional

Frosting:
1 8-oz. package cream cheese, softened
4 cups (1 lb.) powdered sugar
¼ cup butter, softened
1 tsp. vanilla
¼ cup flaked coconut, toasted
Pecan halves, optional

Let eggs stand at room temperature for 30 minutes. Cream together butter, shortening, and sugar until light and fluffy. Add egg yolks and beat well. Stir in vanilla. Combine flour and baking soda; add to creamed mixture alternately with buttermilk, beating well after each addition. Stir in coconut and pecans. In a separate bowl, with clean beaters, beat egg whites until stiff peaks form; gently fold into batter. Pour into two greased and floured 9-inch round pans. Bake at 325° for 40–45 minutes or until toothpick comes out clean. Cool for 10 minutes before removing from pans. Cool completely.

For frosting, beat the cream cheese, sugar, butter, and vanilla until smooth and creamy. Spread between layers and over top and sides of cake. Sprinkle with coconut; garnish with pecans. Store in refrigerator.

Apple Cake

3 T. butter, softened
1 cup sugar
1 egg
1 tsp. vanilla
1 cup flour
1 tsp. baking soda
½ tsp. salt

½ tsp. cinnamon
½ tsp. nutmeg
3 cups diced and peeled
   apples
¼ cup chopped nuts
whipped cream or ice cream,
   optional

Cream butter and sugar until light and fluffy. Beat in egg and vanilla. Combine dry ingredients and then add to creamed mixture (batter will be thick). Stir in apples and nuts. Spread into a greased 8-inch square pan. Bake at 350° for 35–45 minutes or until toothpick comes out with just a few crumbs. Serve warm or cold with whipped cream or ice cream if desired.

Happiness is not in doing what you like, but in liking what you do.

Chocolate Apple Cake

2 cups flour
⅓ cup cocoa powder
1 tsp. baking powder
1 tsp. baking soda
⅔ cup butter, softened
1¼ cups sugar
2 large eggs
1 tsp. vanilla extract
⅔ cup milk

2 medium Granny Smith
   apples, peeled and finely
   chopped

Icing:
3 cups powdered sugar
¼ cup butter, softened
¼ cup cocoa powder
⅓ cup milk

Mix dry ingredients. Beat together butter and sugar until light and fluffy. Add eggs one at a time, beating well after each addition. Beat in vanilla. At low speed, alternately beat flour mixture and milk into butter mixture. Stir in apples. Pour into greased and floured 8-inch square pan. Bake at 350° for 45–55 minutes or until toothpick comes out clean. Cool 10 minutes. Remove from pan and cool completely. For icing, combine first 3 ingredients. Add milk. Spread over top and sides of cake.

Anger is the wind that blows out the lamp of the mind.

CANDIES

Abe Troyer didn't have an electrical license, but his Englisch *neighbor wanted the work done cheap.*
"You have to turn off the juice before any work is done," the neighbor informed him. So Abe called the power company. "I want the juice turned off tomorrow," he said, and the power company agreed. Tomorrow came, and no power company showed up, so Abe called again. "We couldn't find the address," the power company said, and so Abe gave them careful directions. When no one arrived on the next day, Abe called again. "If you don't come this time," he said. "I'll unscrew all the light bulbs and let the juice run out myself."

Caramel Corn

2 sticks butter
2 cups brown sugar
½ cup light corn syrup
½ tsp. salt

½ tsp. vanilla
½ tsp. baking soda
7 quarts popped popcorn

Bring the first four ingredients to a boil. Cook for 5 minutes.
Remove from heat. Add vanilla and baking soda. Pour over
popcorn; mix well. Place in greased roasting pan and bake at
250° for 50 minutes, stirring every 10 minutes.

Saltine Toffee Bark

40 saltine crackers
1 cup butter
¾ cup sugar

2 cups (12 oz.) semisweet
   chocolate chips
1 8-oz. package milk chocolate
   English toffee bits

Line a 15 x 10-inch cookie sheet with heavy duty aluminum
foil. Arrange saltines in a single layer on foil; set aside. In a large
saucepan over medium heat, melt butter. Stir in sugar. Bring to
a boil; cook and stir for 1–2 minutes or until sugar is dissolved.
Pour evenly over crackers. Bake at 350° for 8–10 minutes or until
bubbly. Immediately sprinkle with chocolate chips. Allow chips
to soften for a few minutes, then spread over top. Sprinkle with
toffee bits. Cool.

Cover and refrigerate 1 hour or until set. Break into pieces.
Enjoy!

*Listening is
fifty percent
of our
education.*

Triple Chocolate Fudge

4 tsp. plus ½ cup butter, divided

4½ cups sugar

1 12-oz. can evaporated milk

1 tsp. salt

16 oz. German sweet chocolate, chopped

2 cups (12 oz.) semisweet chocolate chips

1 package (11½ oz.) milk chocolate chips

2 jars (7 oz. each) marshmallow crème

4 cups chopped pecans or walnuts, toasted

2 tsp. vanilla

Don't worry about the business outlook. Be on the outlook for business.

Line two 13 x 9-inch pans with foil and grease the foil with 4 teaspoons butter. In a heavy Dutch oven, combine the sugar, milk, salt, and the remaining butter. Bring to a boil over medium heat, stirring constantly. Cook, without stirring, until candy thermometer reads 234° (soft-ball stage). Remove from the heat. Add the German sweet chocolate and the chocolate chips and stir until smooth. Fold in the marshmallow crème, pecans, and vanilla. Spread into prepared pans. Refrigerate 1 hour or until firm. Using foil, lift fudge out of pan. Discard foil; cut fudge into small pieces and store in airtight container.

Sweet Crispix Mix

1 box (12 oz.) Crispix cereal

½ lb. pecan halves

½ can (use about 6 oz.) deluxe mixed nuts

1 cup small pretzel rings

1 cup cheese crackers

1 cup butter

½ cup light corn syrup

2 cups brown sugar

½ tsp. baking soda

pinch cream of tartar

Heat oven to 300°. Spray two baking sheets with nonstick cooking spray. In a large bowl, mix cereal, pecans, mixed nuts, pretzels, and cheese crackers. Set aside.

Melt butter; stir in the corn syrup and brown sugar. Cook mixture for 5 minutes, stirring constantly. Take off heat and stir in the baking soda and cream of tartar. Carefully pour hot mixture over cereal, stirring with a wooden spoon to coat all ingredients. Divide mixture evenly on both baking sheets. Bake for 15 minutes, stirring twice. Let mixture cool on baking sheets and break apart. If mix is too sticky after cooling, bake 5 or 10 minutes longer.

Susan's Christmas Buckeyes

From *Missing Your Smile*

Laura was smiling now. "Oh, that's so good of you. Do you have any suggestions?"

Susan shrugged. "There are several good possibilities. Russian tea cakes are an Amish specialty. And buckeyes of course…"

Laura laughed. "Wonderful! You're an angel…"

2 lbs. peanut butter (Smucker's Natural Creamy peanut butter)	3 lbs. powdered sugar
1 lb. butter, softened	2–2½ lbs. milk chocolate or candy coating, melted

Mix peanut butter and butter with mixer. Add powdered sugar and mix well. It gets very hard to mix, so use your hands and mix very, very well. Shape into 1–1½-inch balls. Dip each ball into chocolate with toothpick. Don't cover completely so that they will look like a buckeye.

Great leaders take joy in the success of those under them.

Pecan Delights

2¼ cups brown sugar
1 cup butter
1 cup light corn syrup
⅛ tsp. salt
1 14-oz. can sweetened
    condensed milk
1 tsp. vanilla

1½ lbs. whole pecans
1 cup (6 oz.) semisweet
    chocolate chips
1 cup (6 oz.) milk chocolate
    chips
2 T. shortening

In a large saucepan, combine the first four ingredients. Cook over medium heat until all sugar is dissolved. Gradually add milk and mix well. Continue cooking until candy thermometer reads 248°. (I usually don't heat it to this temperature; more like 210° or a bit higher.) Remove from heat; stir in vanilla until blended. Fold in the pecans. Drop by tablespoonfuls onto waxed paper-lined cookie sheet. Chill until firm. Melt chocolate chips and shortening. Drizzle over each cluster. Use sparingly so there's enough chocolate to drizzle on all. Cool. Yield: about 4 dozen.

The soul could have no rainbow if the eyes had no tears.

Chocolate Caramel Candy

1 cup (6 oz.) milk chocolate
    chips
¼ cup butterscotch chips
¼ cup creamy peanut butter

Filling:
¼ cup butter
1 cup sugar
¼ cup evaporated milk
1½ cups marshmallow crème
¼ cup creamy peanut butter
1 tsp. vanilla

1½ cups chopped salted
    peanuts

Caramel Layer:
1 14-oz. package caramels
¼ cup whipping cream

Icing:
1 cup (6 oz.) milk chocolate
    chips
¼ cup butterscotch chips
¼ cup creamy peanut butter

Combine the first three ingredients in a small saucepan; stir over low heat until melted and smooth. Spread onto the bottom of a lightly greased 13 x 9-inch pan. Refrigerate until set.

For filling: Melt butter in a heavy saucepan. Add sugar and milk. Bring to a boil; boil and stir for 5 minutes. Remove from heat; stir in marshmallow crème, peanut butter, and vanilla. Add peanuts. Spread over first layer. Refrigerate until set.

For caramel layer: Combine caramels and cream in a saucepan. Stir over low heat until melted and smooth. Spread over the filling. Refrigerate until set.

For icing: Combine chips and peanut butter; stir over low heat until melted and smooth. Pour over the caramel layer. Refrigerate for at least 1 hour. Cut into 1-inch squares. Store in the refrigerator. Yield: about 8 dozen.

It's not the revolutions that destroy the machinery, it's the friction.

Perfect Peppermint Patties

1 1-lb. box (about 3¾ cups) powdered sugar	¼ cup evaporated milk
3 T. butter, softened	2 cups (12 oz.) semisweet chocolate chips
2–3 tsp. peppermint extract	2 T. shortening
½ tsp. vanilla	

Combine first four ingredients. Add milk and mix well. Roll into 1-inch balls and place on a waxed paper-lined cookie sheet. Chill for 20 minutes. Flatten with a glass to ¼-inch thick; chill for 30 minutes. Melt chocolate chips and shortening. Dip patties; place on waxed paper to harden. Yield: about 5 dozen.

Creamy Caramels

1 cup sugar
1 cup dark corn syrup
1 cup butter

1 14-oz. can sweetened
  condensed milk
1 tsp. vanilla

Line an 8-inch square pan with foil, and butter the foil; set aside. Combine sugar, corn syrup, and butter in a saucepan. Bring to a boil over medium heat, stirring constantly. Boil slowly for 4 minutes without stirring. Remove from the heat and stir in milk. Reduce heat to medium-low and cook until candy thermometer reads 238°, stirring constantly. Remove from the heat and stir in vanilla. Pour into prepared pan. Cool. Remove from pan and cut into 1-inch squares. Wrap individually in waxed paper; twist ends. Yield: 64 pieces.

If heaven is so beautiful on a starry night, what must it be like on the other side?

Coffee Shop Fudge

1 cup chopped pecans
3 cups (18 oz.) semisweet
  chocolate chips
1 14-oz. can sweetened
  condensed milk

2 T. strong brewed coffee,
  room temperature
1 tsp. cinnamon
⅛ tsp. salt
1 tsp. vanilla

Line an 8-inch square pan with foil, and butter the foil; set aside.

Place pecans in a glass pie plate. Microwave, uncovered, on high for 4 minutes, stirring after each minute; set aside. In glass bowl, combine chocolate chips, milk, coffee, cinnamon, and salt. Microwave, uncovered, on high for 1½ minutes. Stir until smooth. Stir in vanilla and pecans. Immediately spread into prepared pan. Cover and refrigerate until firm, about two hours. Remove from pan; cut into 1-inch squares. Cover and store at room temperature.

Chocolate Pecan Caramels

1 T. plus 1 cup butter,
softened, divided
1½ cups pecans, coarsely
chopped and toasted
1 cup (6 oz.) semisweet
chocolate chips

2 cups brown sugar
1 cup light corn syrup
¼ cup water
1 14-oz. can sweetened
condensed milk
2 tsp. vanilla

Line a 13 x 9-inch pan with foil; butter the foil with 1 tablespoon butter. Sprinkle with pecans and chocolate chips; set aside. In a heavy saucepan, melt remaining butter. Add brown sugar, corn syrup, and water. Cook and stir until mixture comes to a boil. Stir in milk and vanilla. Cook, stirring constantly, until a candy thermometer reads 248°. Pour into prepared pan (do not scrape saucepan). Cool completely before cutting.

*Nothing
is more
beautiful
than
cheerfulness
on an old
face.*

Macadamia Almond Brittle

1 cup sugar
½ cup light corn syrup
¾ cup coarsely chopped
macadamia nuts
¾ cup coarsely chopped
almonds

1 T. butter
2 tsp. vanilla
1 tsp. baking soda

Combine sugar and corn syrup in glass bowl. Microwave on high for 5 minutes. Stir in nuts. Microwave on high for 4–5 minutes or until candy thermometer reads 300°. Quickly stir in butter, vanilla, and baking soda until mixture is light and foamy. When bubbles subside, pour onto greased cookie sheet, spreading as thinly as possible with a metal spatula. Cool completely; break into pieces.

Cinnamon Peanut Brittle

1 cup sugar
½ cup light corn syrup
2 cups salted peanuts
1 tsp. butter

½ tsp. cinnamon
1 tsp. baking soda
1 tsp. vanilla

In a glass bowl, combine sugar and corn syrup. Microwave uncovered on high for 4 minutes; stir. Microwave 3 minutes longer. Stir in peanuts, butter, and cinnamon. Microwave uncovered on high for 30–60 seconds or until mixture turns a light amber color. Quickly stir in baking soda and vanilla until light and foamy. Immediately pour into a greased baking sheet and spread with metal spatula. Refrigerate for 20 minutes or until firm; break into small pieces.

Everything in the home today seems to be run by switches, except children.

Easy Popcorn Balls

2 cups sugar
1 cup light corn syrup
1 cup water

3 T. butter
2 quarts salted popcorn

Cook sugar, corn syrup, water, and butter in saucepan to 260° degrees. Pour over popcorn. Mix thoroughly; shape into balls.

COOKIES
AND BARS

*Signs for an Amish mother that your
teenaged boy might be in trouble:*

*1. It's Saturday afternoon and the
deacon's buggy just drove in the lane.*

*2. You rush to his bedroom to discover
colorful socks in the dresser drawer.*

*3. You hear soft music coming
from the hay mow.*

4. He has addressed you in Englisch.

*5. You opened the barn door and heard him
whistling* Yankee Doodle *to the cows.*

6. He is waxing the dashboard of his buggy.

*7. He forgot to take his sister home
from the hymn singing.*

*8. He wants to name his new
driving horse* Camaro.

*9. He claims the Bishop's daughters are
watching the house with field binoculars.*

10. He's wearing his straw hat backwards.

Frosted Banana Bars

½ cup butter, softened
2 cups sugar
3 eggs
1½ cups mashed ripe bananas
1 tsp. vanilla
2 cups flour
1 tsp. baking soda
pinch of salt

Frosting:
½ cup butter, softened
1 8-oz. package cream cheese, softened
4 cups powdered sugar
2 tsp. vanilla

Cream butter and sugar. Beat in eggs, bananas, and vanilla. In a separate bowl combine flour, soda, and salt. Add to creamed mixture and mix well. Pour into greased 15 x 10-inch baking pan. Bake at 350° for 25 minutes or until toothpick inserted near the center comes out clean. Cool. For frosting, cream together the butter and cream cheese. Gradually add powdered sugar, and then add vanilla. Frost bars.

Our fathers teach us what we should become, our mothers teach us what we are.

Butterscotch Brownies

¼ cup shortening
1 cup brown sugar
1 egg
1 tsp. vanilla

¾ cup flour
1 tsp. baking powder
½ tsp. salt
½ cup walnuts

Heat shortening over low heat until melted. Remove from heat. Mix in brown sugar, egg, and vanilla. Stir in remaining ingredients. Spread into greased 8 x 8-inch square pan. Bake at 350° for 25 minutes. Cut into squares while still warm. Variation: Decrease vanilla to ½ teaspoon; stir in ½ cup chopped dates.

Coconut Chews

Crust:
¾ cup powdered sugar
6 T. shortening
6 T. butter, softened
1½ cups flour

Filling:
2 eggs
1 cup brown sugar
2 T. flour
½ tsp. salt

½ tsp. baking powder
½ tsp. vanilla
½ cup chopped walnuts or
   pecans
½ cup flaked coconut

Frosting (if desired):
2 T. butter, melted
3 T. orange juice
1 tsp. lemon juice
1½ cups powdered sugar

*Faith is not
an end but
a means.*

Mix powdered sugar and shortening. Stir in flour. Press into an ungreased 13 x 9-inch pan and bake at 350° for 12–15 minutes, until golden brown. Mix filling ingredients and pour on top of crust. Bake for 20 minutes. If desired, mix frosting ingredients and frost bars when cool.

Chocolate Pecan Brownies

¾ cup flour
¼ tsp. baking soda
¾ cup sugar
⅓ cup butter
2 T. water

1 12-oz. package semisweet
   chocolate morsels
1 tsp. vanilla
2 large eggs
½ cup chopped pecans

Mix flour and baking soda; set aside. In a small saucepan, combine sugar, butter, and water. Bring to a boil and remove from heat immediately. Stir in 1 cup chocolate chips and vanilla. Stir until chocolate is melted and mixture is smooth. Cool completely. Add eggs one at a time, beating well after each one. Gradually stir in the flour mixture until smooth. Stir in remaining chocolate morsels and pecans. Pour into a greased 9-inch square pan and bake at 325° for 30–35 minutes or until toothpick inserted near middle comes out clean.

White Chocolate Blondies

1 cup butter
2¼ cups flour
1½ tsp. baking powder
1 tsp. salt
1½ cups brown sugar
3 eggs

2½ tsp. vanilla
¾ cup chopped macadamia nuts
8 oz. coarsely chopped white chocolate
1 cup dried cranberries

Line a 13 x 9-inch pan with foil and coat with cooking spray. Melt butter. Cook until golden brown, 3–5 minutes. Watch carefully to make sure it doesn't burn. Remove from heat and let cool. Mix flour, baking powder, and salt. Combine cooled butter and sugar. Add eggs one at a time and beat until light and fluffy. Add vanilla. Add flour mixture, nuts, chocolate, and cranberries. Mix until well blended. Spread mixture in pan. Bake at 350° for 25 to 30 minutes. Cool completely before cutting into squares.

Lemon Squares

1 cup flour	1 cup sugar
½ cup butter, softened	½ tsp. baking powder
¼ cup powdered sugar	¼ tsp. salt
2 eggs	2 T. lemon juice

Mix flour, butter, and powdered sugar. Press into ungreased 8 x 8-inch pan, building up ½-inch edges. Bake at 350° for 20 minutes. Beat remaining ingredients until light and fluffy, about 3 minutes. Pour over hot crust. Bake about 25 minutes. These are the best lemon bars ever!

He that seeks God has already found Him.

Tina's Yummy Monster Cookies

12 eggs	1 lb. butter, melted
2 lbs. brown sugar	6 cups peanut butter
4 cups sugar	1 lb. chocolate chips
1 T. vanilla	1 lb. M&Ms
1 T. light corn syrup	18 cups quick oats
8 tsp. baking soda	

Mix in order given. Drop by tablespoonfuls on ungreased cookie sheets. Bake at 350° for 12–14 minutes. Do not overbake. Cool for 1 minute then remove from pan. You may put this dough in the refrigerator until you are ready to bake them (1 or 2 days).

Peanut Butter Cookies

2 cups flour
1 tsp. baking soda
¾ tsp. baking powder
¾ cup butter, softened
¾ cup chunky peanut butter

¾ cup sugar
¾ cup brown sugar
2 eggs
1 tsp. vanilla

Mix flour, soda, baking powder, and salt. Beat together butter, peanut butter, and sugars at medium speed until light and fluffy. Beat in eggs and vanilla. Gradually beat in flour mixture at low speed. Wrap dough in plastic wrap; chill for 2 hours or overnight.

Preheat oven to 375°. Grease two baking sheets. Roll level tablespoons of dough into balls. Place cookies on baking sheets. Using tines of a fork dipped in sugar or flour, lightly press a crisscross pattern onto each cookie. Bake until golden, 9–12 minutes. Cool 1 minute before removing from baking sheet.

Sour Cream Cookies

½ cup butter
1½ cups brown sugar
2 eggs
¼ tsp. maple flavoring
1 tsp. vanilla
1 tsp. baking soda
3 cups flour
½ tsp. baking powder
¼ tsp. salt

1 cup sour cream
½ cup nuts

Frosting:
1 cup brown sugar
¼ cup cream or evaporated milk
1 stick (½ cup) butter
2 cups powdered sugar

Cream together the butter and sugar. Add eggs and flavorings. Add dry ingredients to creamed mixture. Add sour cream and nuts. Bake at 350° for 13 minutes. For frosting, cook brown sugar, cream, and butter. Add powdered sugar. Frost cookies when cool.

Banana Oatmeal Cookies

1 cup butter-flavored
    shortening
1 cup sugar
2 eggs
1 tsp. vanilla
2 cups flour
1 tsp. baking soda

1 tsp. cinnamon
1 tsp. cloves
3 medium bananas, mashed
2 cups quick-cooking oats
1 cup (6 ounces) semisweet
    chocolate chips

In a large bowl, cream together the shortening and sugar until light and fluffy. Beat in eggs and vanilla. Combine flour, baking soda, cinnamon, and cloves. Add to creamed mixture and mix well. Stir in bananas, oats, and chocolate chips. Drop by teaspoonfuls onto greased baking sheets. Bake at 375° for 10 to 12 minutes. Immediately remove from cookie sheet and cool.

Mini Cinnamon Roll Cookies

1 cup butter, softened
1¾ cups sugar, divided
3 egg yolks
1 T. plus 1 tsp. honey, divided
1 tsp. vanilla
2½ cups flour

1 tsp. baking powder
½ tsp. salt
½ tsp. cream of tartar
1 T. cinnamon
8 oz. white baking chocolate, chopped

In a large bowl, cream together the butter and 1¼ cups sugar until light and fluffy. Beat in egg yolks, 1 tablespoon honey, and vanilla. Combine the flour, baking powder, salt, and cream of tartar; gradually add to creamed mixture and mix well.

Shape a heaping tablespoonful of dough into a 6-inch log. In a shallow bowl, combine cinnamon and remaining sugar; roll log in cinnamon sugar. Loosely coil log into a spiral shape; place on a greased cookie sheet. Repeat, placing cookies 1 inch apart. Sprinkle with remaining cinnamon sugar. Bake at 350° for 8–10 minutes or until set. Cool completely. Melt white chocolate with remaining honey; stir until smooth. Drizzle over cookies.

Poverty is not a shame unless you are slothful.

Gingerbread Cookies with Buttercream Frosting

⅔ cup shortening
1 cup sugar
1 egg
¼ cup molasses
2 cups flour
1 tsp. baking soda
1 tsp. salt
1 tsp. each cinnamon, cloves, and ginger

Frosting:
3 cups powdered sugar
⅓ cup butter, softened
1 tsp. vanilla
¼ tsp. lemon extract
¼ tsp. butter flavoring
3–4 T. milk

Cream together the shortening and sugar. Beat in egg and molasses. Combine flour, baking soda, salt, and spices; gradually add to the creamed mixture and mix well. Refrigerate for 2 hours or overnight. On a lightly floured surface, roll dough into ¼-inch thickness. Cut into desired shapes. Place on ungreased cookie sheets. Bake at 350° for 8–10 minutes or until edges begin to brown.

For frosting: Beat together the sugar, butter, and flavorings. Gradually add milk until smooth and thick. Frost cooled cookies.

Making no choice when we have to choose is itself a choice.

Cinnamon Oatmeal Cookies

2½ cups shortening
5 cups sugar
4 eggs
⅓ cup molasses
1 T. vanilla
4¾ cups quick-cooking oats

4⅓ cups flour
4 tsp. baking powder
4 tsp. cinnamon
1 tsp. baking soda
1 tsp. salt

Cream together the shortening and sugar. Add eggs, one at a time, beating well after each addition. Beat in molasses and vanilla. Combine remaining ingredients; gradually add to creamed mixture. Drop by tablespoonfuls on greased cookie sheets. Bake at 350° for 10–12 minutes or until edges are firm. Yields about 13 dozen cookies.

Old-Fashioned Sugar Cookies

2 cups brown sugar
2 cups sugar
2 cups oil
4 eggs
2 cups buttermilk
4 tsp. baking powder

2 tsp. baking soda
7 cups flour
2 tsp. vanilla
a couple drops lemon
    flavoring
sugar

Cream together sugars and oil. Add eggs. Mix dry ingredients and add alternately with buttermilk. Add flavorings. Chill several hours or overnight. Drop on greased cookie sheet, sprinkle tops with sugar, and bake at 400° for 8 minutes.

These are the cookies Mom would serve the children in our Amish church.

*The best
time to
praise a
man is
when he
isn't there.*

Ice Box Date Cookies

1 lb. dates, cut fine
2 cups sugar, divided
1 cup cool water
1 cup brown sugar
1 cup butter and lard mixed

3 well beaten eggs
4 cups flour
¾ tsp. salt
1 tsp. baking soda
1 tsp. vanilla

Boil dates, 1 cup sugar, and water until thick. While this is cooking, prepare dough. Cream together the butter, lard, 1 cup sugar, and brown sugar. Add eggs. Mix dry ingredients and add to egg mixture along with vanilla. Divide dough. Roll out and spread date mixture on. Roll up as you would a jelly roll. Refrigerate. Slice and bake at 375° until brown.

Choco-Cloud Brownies

1 cup butter, softened (no
   substitutes)
2 cups sugar
4 eggs
1 milk chocolate candy bar,
   (7 oz.) melted
3 tsp. vanilla
2 cups flour
½ tsp. salt

2 cups chopped pecans
Frosting:
5 T. flour
1 cup milk
1 cup butter
1 cup powdered sugar
2 tsp. vanilla
cocoa

Cream butter and sugar. Add eggs, one at a time, beating
well after each addition. Add chocolate and vanilla; mix well.
Gradually add flour and salt. Stir in pecans. Spread into a
greased 13 x 9-inch pan. Bake at 350° for 35–40 minutes or until
center is set and edges pull away. Cool.

For frosting: Combine flour and milk in a saucepan until
smooth. Bring to a boil; cook and stir for 2 minutes or until
thickened. Remove from heat. Cool completely. Cream together
the butter and powdered sugar. Add vanilla. Mix well. Gradually
add to milk mixture. Beat 5 minutes or until fluffy. Frost; then
dust with cocoa.

White Velvet Cutouts

2 cups butter, softened
1 8-oz. package cream cheese,
   softened
2 cups sugar
2 egg yolks
1 tsp. vanilla extract
4½ cups flour

Frosting:
3½ cups powdered sugar,
   divided
3 T. butter, softened
1 T. shortening
½ tsp. vanilla
3–4 T. milk, divided
Red and/or green food
   coloring, optional

Cream together the butter and cream cheese until light and fluffy. Add sugar, egg yolks, and vanilla; mix well. Gradually add flour. Cover and chill 2 hours or until firm.

Roll out on a floured surface to ¼-inch thickness. Cut into 3-inch shapes; place 1 inch apart on greased baking sheets. Bake at 350° for 10–12 minutes or until set (not browned). Cool 5 minutes; remove from pan and cool completely.

For frosting: Combine 1½ cups powdered sugar, butter, shortening, vanilla, and 3 tablespoons milk; beat until smooth. Gradually add remaining sugar; beat until light and fluffy, about 3 minutes. Add enough remaining milk and food coloring until frosting reaches desired consistency. Frost cookies. Yields about 7 dozen cookies.

Everything
that is
beautiful
has been
loved into
being.

Pumpkin Cookies

1 cup sugar
1 cup canned pumpkin
½ cup shortening
2 cups flour
1 tsp. baking powder
1 tsp. baking soda
1 tsp. cinnamon
¼ tsp. salt

½ cup raisins
½ cup chopped nuts

Light Brown Glaze:
¼ cup butter
2 cups powdered sugar
1 tsp. vanilla
1–2 T. milk

Preheat oven to 375°. Mix sugar, pumpkin, and shortening. Stir in dry ingredients, then fold in raisins and nuts. Drop dough by teaspoonfuls on ungreased cookie sheet. Bake until light brown, 8–10 minutes. Remove from cookie sheet; cool. For glaze, heat butter in saucepan until delicate brown. Stir in powdered sugar and vanilla. Stir in milk until smooth.

Chunky Cookies

½ cup butter, softened
½ cup butter-flavored
    shortening
1 cup brown sugar
¾ cup sugar
2 eggs
2 tsp. vanilla
2½ cups flour

1 tsp. baking soda
⅛ tsp. salt
1 cup miniature semisweet
    chocolate chips
1 cup milk chocolate chips
1 cup vanilla or white chips
4 squares (1 oz. each)
    bittersweet chocolate,
    coarsely chopped

Cream together the butter, shortening, and sugars until light and fluffy. Add eggs, one at a time, beating well after each addition. Beat in vanilla. Combine the flour, baking soda, and salt; gradually add to the creamed mixture. Stir in remaining ingredients. Drop by tablespoonfuls on ungreased baking sheets. Bake at 350° for 10–12 minutes or until lightly browned. Cool for 2–3 minutes before removing from pan.

Amish Whoopie Pies

1½ cups shortening
3 cups sugar
3 eggs, well beaten
1½ cups sour milk
3 tsp. vanilla
1½ cups cocoa
6 cups flour
3 tsp. salt
3 tsp. baking soda
1½ cups hot water

Filling:
3 egg whites
3 tsp. vanilla
6 T. milk
approximately 3 cups
    powdered sugar
1½ cups shortening

Cream together the shortening and sugar. Add eggs, milk, vanilla, flour, cocoa, and salt. Dissolve baking soda in hot water and add to mixture. Drop by teaspoonfuls onto greased cookie sheets. Bake at 375° for 8 minutes or until done.

For filling: Beat egg whites until stiff. Add vanilla, milk, and powdered sugar. Cream shortening and add to mixture. Put filling between 2 cookies.

Pumpkin Whoopie Pies

2 cups brown sugar
1 cup vegetable oil
2 eggs
1½ cups cooked pumpkin
3 cups flour
1 tsp. salt
1 tsp. baking powder
1 tsp. baking soda
1½ tsp. cinnamon

½ tsp. ginger
¼ tsp. cloves
1 tsp. vanilla

Filling:

3 oz. cream cheese
1½ cups shortening
2 cups powdered sugar
2 egg whites, beaten stiff

*If you aim
at nothing,
you're bound
to hit it.*

Cream together the sugar and oil. Add eggs and pumpkin. Add dry ingredients and vanilla. Mix well. Drop by teaspoonful on greased cookie sheets. Bake at 350° for 10–12 minutes. Cool.

Beat together the cream cheese and shortening. Add powdered sugar and mix well. Mix in beaten egg whites. Put filling between 2 cookies.

Toffee-Topped Bars

2 cups brown sugar
2 cups flour
½ cup butter, softened
1 tsp. baking powder
½ tsp. salt
1 tsp. vanilla extract

1 cup milk
1 egg
1 cup semisweet chocolate
   chips
½ cup chopped walnuts
¼ cup unsweetened flaked
   coconut (optional)

Mix brown sugar and flour. Cut in butter until mixture resembles coarse crumbs. Remove 1 cup crumbs; set aside. To remaining mixture add baking powder and salt. Using a fork, lightly beat in vanilla, milk, and egg. Continue beating until a smooth batter forms. Pour batter into a lightly greased 13 x 9-inch pan. In a small bowl, combine the chocolate chips and walnuts. Fold in coconut if desired. Sprinkle reserved crumb mixture over top of batter in pan, then sprinkle with the walnuts and chocolate chips. Bake bars at 350° for 35 minutes or until toothpick comes out clean.

Apple-Oatmeal Cookies

1½ cups quick-cooking rolled
   oats
¾ cup flour
¾ cup whole-wheat flour
½ cup brown sugar
1 tsp. baking powder
¼ tsp. baking soda
½ tsp. salt
1½ tsp. cinnamon

½ cup raisins
1 cup finely chopped, peeled
   tart apples
1 egg, slightly beaten
½ cup honey
½ cup oil
⅓ cup milk

Combine oats, flours, brown sugar, baking powder, baking soda, salt, and cinnamon. Stir in raisins and apples. In large bowl, combine egg, honey, oil, and milk. Stir in dry ingredients. Drop by teaspoonfuls onto ungreased cookie sheets. Dip fingers in water; press dough down to about 1½ inches in diameter. Bake at 375° for 10–12 minutes or until lightly golden.

Caramel Creams

1 cup butter (no substitutes)
⅔ cup brown sugar
2 egg yolks
½ tsp. vanilla
2½ cups flour
⅓ cup pecans, finely chopped

¼ tsp. salt

Filling:
2½ T. butter
1½ cups powdered sugar
½ tsp. vanilla
2–3 T. whipping cream

If you walk with God, you will be out of step with the world.

Cream butter and brown sugar. Beat in egg yolks and vanilla. In separate bowl combine flour, pecans, and salt. Gradually add to creamed mixture. Shape dough into two 10-inch rolls. Wrap in plastic wrap and refrigerate for 2 hours. Unwrap and slice each roll into 25–30 cookies. Bake at 350° on an ungreased cookie sheet for 11–13 minutes or until golden. Let cool on a wire rack. For filling, melt butter in saucepan; stir until golden brown. Remove from heat; add powdered sugar, vanilla, and enough cream to achieve spreading consistency. Spread on half of the cookies and top with remaining cookies.

Twelve-Yolk Sugar Cookies

1 cup sugar
1 cup brown sugar
1½ cups butter, softened
12 egg yolks
2 tsp. lemon juice

3½ cups flour
2 tsp. baking soda
½ tsp. salt
extra sugar (for rolling)

Cream sugars and butter. Beat in egg yolks and lemon juice. Add flour, baking soda, and salt; mix well. Chill at least 30 minutes. Form into balls and roll in sugar. Place on greased cookie sheets and flatten with flat bottom of a glass. Bake at 350° for 10 minutes or until lightly browned. Yield: 6 dozen.

This recipe is nice if you have had to use a lot of egg whites for angel food cake.

You begin to slip when you'd rather win an argument than be right.

Cream Wafers

½ cup butter
½ cup sugar
½ cup brown sugar
2 eggs, beaten
2 T. cream
1 tsp. vanilla
2¾ cups flour
1½ tsp. soda

½ tsp. cinnamon
½ tsp. salt

Filling:
4 T. butter
1–2 T. heavy cream
2 cups powdered sugar
1 tsp. vanilla

Cream butter and sugars; add eggs, cream, and vanilla. Mix dry ingredients and add to creamed mixture. Put into cookie press and press onto ungreased cookie sheets. Bake at 350° just until set but not browned. Cool. Mix filling ingredients and sandwich between wafers.

Apricot Pecan Tassies

½ cup plus 1 T. butter,
    softened, divided
6 T. cream cheese, softened
1 cup flour
¾ cup brown sugar

1 egg, lightly beaten
½ tsp. vanilla extract
¼ tsp. salt
⅔ cup diced dried apricots
⅓ cup chopped pecans

Cream ½ cup butter and cream cheese until light and fluffy. Gradually add flour, beating until mixture forms a ball. Cover and refrigerate 15 minutes. Meanwhile, combine brown sugar, egg, vanilla, salt, and remaining 1 tablespoon butter. Stir in apricots and pecans; set aside.

Shape chilled dough into 1-inch balls. Press onto the bottom and up the sides of greased miniature muffin cups. Spoon 1 teaspoon apricot mixture into each cup. Bake at 325° for 25 minutes or until golden brown. Cool in pans.

Big ships can only be launched where the water is deep.

Pecan Crescent Cookies

1 cup butter, softened
½ cup sugar
1 tsp. vanilla extract

2 cups flour
1 cup finely chopped pecans
powdered sugar

Cream the butter, sugar, and vanilla until light and fluffy. Gradually add flour. Stir until smooth, then fold in pecans. Shape rounded teaspoonfuls of dough into 2½-inch logs and curve into crescents. Place 1 inch apart on ungreased baking sheets. Bake at 325° for 20–22 minutes or until set and bottoms are lightly browned. Let stand 2–3 minutes before removing from pans. Dust with powdered sugar just before serving.

Triple-Nut Diamonds

1 cup flour
½ cup sugar
½ cup cold butter, divided
½ cup brown sugar

2 T. honey
¼ cup heavy whipping cream
⅔ cup each chopped pecans,
  walnuts, and almonds

Preheat oven to 350°. Line a 9-inch square pan with foil; grease the foil and set aside. Combine the flour and sugar in medium bowl. Cut in ¼ cup butter until mixture resembles coarse crumbs. Press into prepared pan and bake for 10 minutes.

In a saucepan, heat the brown sugar, honey, and ¼ cup remaining butter until bubbly. Boil for 1 minute. Remove from heat; stir in cream and nuts. Pour over crust. Bake 16–20 minutes longer or until surface is bubbly. Cool and refrigerate 30 minutes. Using foil, lift bars out of the pan and cut into diamonds.

Pecan Squares

2 cups flour
⅓ cup sugar
¼ tsp. salt
¾ cup cold butter

Filling:
4 eggs, lightly beaten
1½ cups light corn syrup
1½ cups sugar
3 T. butter, melted
1½ tsp. vanilla extract
2½ cups chopped pecans

Combine flour, sugar, and salt. Cut in butter until mixture resembles coarse crumbs. Press firmly and evenly into a greased 15 x 10-inch pan. Bake at 350° for 20 minutes.

For filling, combine the eggs, corn syrup, sugar, butter, and vanilla. Stir in pecans. Spread evenly over hot crust. Bake 25–30 minutes longer or until set. Cool.

Best Cake Brownies

½ cup butter, softened
1 cup sugar
4 eggs
1 can (16 oz.) chocolate syrup
1 tsp. vanilla extract
1 cup flour
½ tsp. salt

Glaze:
1 cup sugar
⅓ cup butter
⅓ cup milk
⅔ cup semisweet chocolate chips
⅔ cup miniature marshmallows

Cream butter and sugar until light and fluffy. Add the eggs, one at a time, beating well after each addition. Beat in chocolate syrup and vanilla. Add the flour and salt until blended. Pour into greased 15 x 10-inch pan. Bake at 350° for 20–25 minutes or until toothpick comes out clean (top of brownies will still appear wet). Cool for 15–20 minutes.

For glaze, combine sugar, butter, and milk in a saucepan. Bring to a boil; boil until the sugar is dissolved. Remove from the heat; add chocolate chips and marshmallows and stir until melted. Pour over the brownies and spread evenly with an offset spatula. Refrigerate for 5 minutes before cutting.

Give some people an inch and they want to be rulers.

Russian Teacakes

1 cup butter, softened
½ cup powdered sugar
1 tsp. vanilla
2¼ cups flour

¼ tsp. salt
¾ cup finely chopped nuts
powdered sugar

Mix butter, powdered sugar, and vanilla in large bowl. Mix in flour, salt, and nuts until dough holds together. Shape into 1-inch balls and place about 1 inch apart on ungreased cookie sheets.

Bake at 400° for 10–12 minutes until set but not brown. Roll in powdered sugar while warm; cool. Roll in powdered sugar again before serving.

Fudgy Nut Brownies

2½ cups semisweet chocolate
    chips
1 cup butter
1 cup sugar
¼ tsp. salt
4 eggs
2 tsp. vanilla extract
¾ cup flour
1 cup coarsely chopped
    hazelnuts or almonds,
    toasted

Topping:
12 squares (1 oz. each)
    semisweet chocolate
1 T. shortening
3 squares (1 oz. each) white
    baking chocolate

Times which are especially trying are times for trying.

Melt chocolate chips and butter in saucepan over low heat; stir until smooth. Combine sugar and salt in medium bowl; pour chocolate over sugar. Stir until smooth and let cool for 10 minutes. Stir in eggs, vanilla, flour, and nuts. Spread into a greased 15 x 10-inch pan. Bake at 350° for 25–30 minutes or until toothpick comes out with moist crumbs (do not overbake). Cool. For topping, melt semisweet chocolate and shortening; stir until smooth. Spread over brownies. Melt white chocolate; cool slightly. Pour into a resealable plastic bag. Pipe thin lines 1 inch apart. Gently pull a toothpick through the lines from the opposite direction.

Chocolate-Oat Squares

¾ cup butter, melted
1¼ cups brown sugar
1½ cups flour
1½ cups old-fashioned
    rolled oats
1 tsp. baking soda
¼ tsp. salt

Glaze:
9 oz. semisweet chocolate or
    milk chocolate, cut into
    small pieces
5 T. heavy cream

Melt butter and pour over brown sugar. Stir to combine. In separate bowl, mix together flour, oats, baking soda, and salt. Add dry ingredients into sugar mixture and stir until combined. Spread in a greased 13 x 9-inch pan and pat into an even layer. Bake at 350° until lightly browned, about 15 minutes. Cool completely.

For glaze, melt chocolate in small saucepan over low heat. Stir in cream. Spread over bars with offset spatula and chill until chocolate is set, about 30 minutes.

Chewy Chocolate Cookies

2 cups flour
⅓ cup unsweetened cocoa
1 tsp. baking powder
pinch salt
1½ cups butter, softened

1 cup brown sugar
1 cup sugar
2 large eggs
1 tsp. vanilla extract
1½ cups finely chopped
    almonds (about 6 oz.)

Mix flour, cocoa, baking powder, and salt. In separate bowl, cream butter and sugars until light and fluffy. Add eggs one at a time, beating well after each addition. Beat in vanilla. At low speed, gradually beat flour mixture into egg mixture until well blended. Stir in nuts. Drop by rounded teaspoonfuls onto greased cookie sheets. Bake at 350° for 10–12 minutes, until just set. Cool slightly; remove from pan.

Mose Stutzman went to the banker in town as a last desperate move to purchase the spring's harvest seed.
"What do you have as collateral?" the banker asked.
"What is collateral?" Mose asked.
"That's something you agree to give me to sell in case you lose my money," the banker replied.
"You can have my prize set of Belgians," Mose said.
"That'll be perfect," the banker agreed, and Mose got his loan.
Six months later, Mose was back. He repaid the loan with interest, all of it with cash. Seeing the wad of bills left over, the banker asked Mose, "Would you like to deposit the extra cash for safekeeping? We pay a small amount of interest."
Mose thought for a moment and then said, "What have you got for collateral?"

DESSERTS

*A politician unfamiliar with the
Amish ways stopped in at Henry
Mullet's place. He walked up
to young Luke, who was busy
milking the cow out by the barn.
Before the politician could get many
words out of his mouth, Henry
opened the front door and hollered
out, "What does he want, Luke?"
"He's a politician," Luke said.
"Well then, get in the house at
once and bring the cow with
you," Henry hollered back.*

Caramel Rhubarb Cobbler

7 T. butter, divided
¾ cup brown sugar
½ cup sugar, divided
3 T. cornstarch
1¼ cups water
6 cups chopped fresh or
    frozen rhubarb, thawed
3–4 drops red food coloring,
    optional

1¼ cups flour
1½ tsp. baking powder
¼ tsp. salt
⅓ cup milk
cinnamon sugar, optional
whipped cream or ice cream,
    optional

Melt 3 tablespoons butter. Pour into bowl and add brown sugar, ¼ cup sugar, and cornstarch. Gradually stir in water and rhubarb; cook, stirring, until thickened, about 5–8 minutes. Add food coloring if desired. Pour into a greased 2-quart baking dish and set aside. Combine flour, baking powder, salt, and remaining ¼ cup sugar. Melt remaining 4 tablespoons butter; add to dry ingredients with milk. Mix well. Drop by tablespoonfuls onto rhubarb mixture. Bake at 350° for 35–40 minutes or until the fruit is bubbly and the top is golden brown. Sprinkle with cinnamon sugar if desired. Serve warm with whipped cream or ice cream if desired.

Little and often make much.

Ice Cream Dessert

1 package chocolate sandwich
    cookies, crushed
1 cup margarine, divided
½ gallon vanilla ice cream,
    softened
1½ cups chopped peanuts
2 cups powdered sugar

1 12-oz. can evaporated milk
⅔ cup semisweet chocolate
    chips
1 tsp. vanilla extract

Crush cookies and place in large bowl. Melt ½ cup margarine and pour over cookies. Toss to combine. Press into a 13 x 9-inch pan and freeze until cold. Spread softened ice cream over cold crust and freeze until set. Sprinkle with chopped nuts. Combine sugar, evaporated milk, chocolate chips, remaining ½ cup margarine, and vanilla in large saucepan and bring to boil over medium heat. Boil for 7 minutes, stirring constantly. Watch this very closely. Remove and cool. Pour over peanuts and sprinkle a few chopped nuts on top for garnish. Freeze until set. Serves 24.

Cherry Cheese Delight

1 sleeve graham crackers, crushed

⅓ cup butter, melted

1 8-oz. package cream cheese, softened

¾ cup powdered sugar, divided

1 T. milk

½ tsp. almond extract, divided

½ cup chopped pecans

1 cup heavy cream

1 can cherry pie filling

½ tsp. almond extract, divided

Combine crackers and butter and press into bottom of 9-inch square pan. Combine cream cheese, ½ cup powdered sugar, milk, and ¼ teaspoon almond extract. Spread onto crust and sprinkle with pecans. Refrigerate. Whip cream and add remaining ¼ cup powdered sugar. Spread over pecans.

Combine pie filling and remaining ¼ teaspoon almond extract; spread over whipped cream layer. Chill several hours or overnight.

Sara's Date Pudding

Cake:
1 cup boiling water
1 cup dates, chopped
1 tsp. baking soda
1 cup sugar
1 cup flour
1 T. butter, melted
½ cup nuts
1 tsp. vanilla
¼ tsp. salt
1 egg

Pudding:
1 cup brown sugar
⅔ cup water
2 T. butter
1 tsp. baking soda
2 tsp. vanilla
2 egg yolks
2 T. flour
2 T. cornstarch
3 cups milk

Toppings:
whipped topping
bananas, sliced

A narrow mind and a wide mouth usually go together.

For cake, pour 1 cup boiling water over dates and soda. Let cool, then mix in remaining ingredients. Pour into a greased 13 x 9-inch pan. Bake at 350° for 30 minutes and let cool. Once cake is cooled, cut into small cubes.

For pudding, put brown sugar, water, butter, soda, and vanilla in saucepan and cook over medium heat for 10 minutes. Remove from heat and stir in egg yolks, flour, cornstarch, and milk. Heat and stir until thickened. Cool.

Layer in glass bowl cake, pudding, whipped topping, and bananas. Repeat with as many layers as desired.

Peach-Apricot Cobbler

½ cup sugar

2 T. cornstarch

1 can (1 lb. 13 oz.) sliced peaches, drained, juice reserved

1 can (10½ oz.) apricot halves, drained, juice reserved

1 T. butter

½ tsp. cinnamon

¼ tsp. nutmeg

Topping:

½ cup flour

½ cup sugar

¾ tsp. baking powder

¼ tsp. salt

2 T. butter, softened

1 large egg

Garnish:

1 cup heavy cream

2 T. honey

½ tsp. cinnamon

Difficulties were meant to make us better, not bitter.

Preheat oven to 400°. In a saucepan, mix sugar and cornstarch. Stir in ½ cup of each of the reserved juices. Cook, stirring constantly, until mixture boils and thickens, 2 minutes. Remove from heat. Stir in butter, cinnamon, and nutmeg. Add fruit and toss gently to combine. Spoon into a 1½-quart casserole dish.

To prepare topping, mix together flour, sugar, baking powder, salt, butter, and egg. Spoon topping over fruit mixture. Bake cobbler until topping is lightly golden, 30 minutes. To prepare garnish, beat heavy cream, honey, and cinnamon at medium speed until soft peaks form. Serve cobbler warm, topped with garnish.

Note: Use any combination of canned fruit: plums, pears, pineapple, or mandarin oranges.

Lava Cakes

4 tsp. sugar
½ cup butter
4 oz. semisweet chocolate,
    chopped
1 cup powdered sugar
2 eggs plus 2 egg yolks
1½ tsp. instant coffee granules
¾ tsp. vanilla extract
6 T. flour
½ tsp. salt
whipped cream, optional
additional powdered sugar,
    optional

Grease the bottom and sides of four 6-oz. ramekins; sprinkle each with 1 tsp. sugar. Place ramekins on a baking sheet; set aside.

Melt butter and chocolate over low heat; stir until smooth. Pour into bowl and stir in powdered sugar until smooth. Whisk in the eggs, egg yolks, instant coffee, and vanilla. Stir in flour and salt and mix until smooth. Spoon batter into ramekins.

Bake at 400° for about 12 minutes, or until cake sides are set and centers are soft.

Remove ramekins to a wire rack to cool for 5 minutes. Carefully run a small knife around edge to loosen cake and invert onto serving plates. Lift ramekins off. Serve warm with whipped cream or sprinkle with additional powdered sugar if desired.

*A true friend
will place
a finger on
your faults
without
rubbing
them in.*

Banana Sundae Dessert

1 package (12 oz.) vanilla
    wafers, crushed
½ cup butter, melted
2 T. sugar
6 cups chocolate chip ice
    cream, softened
4 large bananas sliced
2 jars (11¾ oz. each) hot fudge
    ice cream topping, divided
6 cups cherry vanilla ice
    cream, softened
maraschino cherries

In a small bowl, combine the wafer crumbs, butter, and sugar; press into the bottom of a 13 x 9-inch pan. Freeze for 15 minutes until firm. Spread chocolate chip ice cream over crust. Layer with bananas and 1½ cups fudge topping. Cover and freeze for at least 30 minutes. Spread cherry vanilla ice cream evenly over topping. Cover and freeze for 6 hours or overnight. Remove from freezer 10 minutes before serving. Warm remaining fudge topping. Drizzle over each serving; top each with a cherry.

Caramel-Nut Cheesecake

2 cups graham cracker
  crumbs
1 cup chopped peanuts,
  divided
1¼ cups sugar, divided
6 T. butter, melted
4 packages (8 oz. each) cream
  cheese, softened

2 tsp. vanilla
1 cup sour cream
4 eggs
¼ cup caramel ice cream
  topping

Preheat oven to 350°. Line 13 x 9-inch pan with foil extending over sides. Mix crumbs, ½ cup nuts, ¼ cup sugar, and melted butter; press into bottom of pan. Bake 10 minutes. Meanwhile, beat cream cheese, remaining 1 cup sugar, and vanilla with mixer until well blended. Add sour cream; mix well. Add eggs, one at a time, beating after each addition just until combined. Pour over crust. Bake 35 minutes or until center is almost set. Let cool at room temperature for 1 hour, then refrigerate at least 4 hours before serving. Top with remaining nuts and caramel topping. Use foil handles to lift cheesecake from pan before cutting to serve.

White Chocolate Raspberry Torte

¾ cup butter
2 cups sugar
4 eggs
1 cup white chocolate chips,
    melted and cooled
1 tsp. vanilla extract
3 cups cake flour
1 tsp. baking powder
½ tsp. baking soda
1 cup buttermilk

Filling:
2 cups fresh or frozen
    raspberries
¾ cup water
½ cup sugar
3 T. cornstarch

Frosting:
1 package (8 oz.) cream
    cheese, softened
1 cup white chocolate chips,
    melted and cooled
1 carton (12 oz.) whipped
    topping

The more you know, the more you know you don't know.

Cream butter and sugar until light and fluffy. Add eggs, one at a time, beating well after each addition. Beat in melted chocolate and vanilla. Combine flour, baking powder, and baking soda; add to creamed mixture alternately with buttermilk, beating well after each addition. Transfer to two greased and floured 9-inch round pans. Bake at 350° for 28–32 minutes or until toothpick comes out clean. Cool 10 minutes before removing from pans. Cool completely.

In a small saucepan, bring raspberries and water to a boil. Reduce heat and simmer 5 minutes. Remove from heat. Press raspberries through a sieve; discard seeds. Cool. In the same pan, combine sugar and cornstarch. Stir in raspberry puree until smooth. Bring to a boil; cook and stir for 2 minutes or until thickened. Cool. Spread between cake layers. Beat cream cheese until fluffy. Beat in melted chips and fold in whipped topping. Spread over top and sides of cake. Store in refrigerator until ready to serve.

Laura's Rice Custard

4 cups milk
2 cups cooked rice (do not pack)
½ cup raisins
3 eggs

1 cup sugar
½ tsp. salt
1 tsp. vanilla
cinnamon
nutmeg

Heat milk, rice, and raisins in small saucepan until warm. Set aside. In separate bowl, beat egg and whisk in sugar and salt. Add hot milk mixture to eggs along with vanilla. Pour into 2-quart baking dish. Sprinkle with cinnamon and nutmeg. Set in shallow pan of water and bake at 325° for approximately 1 hour. Stir twice while baking—20 minutes after start of baking time and again about 15 minutes later. (This helps to keep rice and raisins from settling.)

Note: Laura is an older lady in our church and she knew I loved her rice custard. She often brought it to carry-ins at church.

The best way to succeed in life is to act on the advice you give others.

Pumpkin Swirl Cheesecake

25 Nabisco gingersnaps, finely crushed (about 1½ cups)
½ cup finely chopped pecans
¼ cup butter, melted
4 packages (8 oz. each) cream cheese, softened
1 cup sugar, divided

1 tsp. vanilla
4 eggs
1 cup canned pumpkin
1 tsp. cinnamon
¼ tsp. nutmeg
dash ground cloves

Preheat oven to 325° (or 300° if using a dark pan). Mix gingersnap crumbs, pecans, and melted butter; press firmly into bottom and 1 inch up the side of 9-inch springform pan. Beat cream cheese, ¾ cup sugar, and vanilla until well blended. Add eggs, one at a time, mixing on low speed after each addition just until blended. Remove 1½ cups plain batter and set aside. Stir remaining ¼ cup sugar, pumpkin, and spices into remaining batter. Spoon half of the pumpkin batter into crust; top with spoonfuls of half of the reserved plain batter. Repeat layers. Cut through batters with knife several times to create a swirl effect. Bake 55 minutes or until center is almost set. Cool completely at room temperature, then refrigerate 4 hours or overnight. Cut into 16 slices.

Raspberry Trifle

1 package (16 oz.) pound cake, cut into 18 slices
2 packages (3.4 oz. each) instant vanilla pudding mix
1 jar (18 oz.) raspberry jam
1½ pints fresh raspberries
whipped cream and fresh raspberries for garnish

Arrange one third of sliced cake on the bottom of a trifle dish or large decorative bowl. Prepare pudding according to package directions. Place another third of the cake pieces around inside of bowl, using half of pudding to hold them in place. Gently stir together jam and raspberries; spoon half over the pudding. Cover with remaining cake pieces. Layer remaining pudding and raspberry mixture. Chill. Garnish with whipped cream and raspberries. Yield: 8–10 servings.

Apple Crisp

4 cups sliced tart apples	½ cup oats
¾ cup brown sugar	¾ tsp. cinnamon
½ cup flour	⅓ cup butter, softened

Heat oven to 375°. Arrange apples in greased 8-inch square pan. Mix all remaining ingredients and sprinkle over apples. Bake until topping is golden brown and apples are tender, about 30 minutes. Serve warm with ice cream or milk.

A rose does not know where her scent reaches, just as a man does not know who his life will touch.

Blueberry Crisp

3 cups blueberries or 1 package (16 oz.) frozen unsweetened blueberries	½ cup quick-cooking oats
	¾ tsp. cinnamon
	¼ tsp. salt
2 T. lemon juice	⅓ cup butter, softened
⅔ cup brown sugar	ice cream or half-and-half (to serve)
½ cup flour	

Heat oven to 375°. Arrange blueberries in ungreased 8-inch square pan. Sprinkle with lemon juice. Mix brown sugar, flour, oats, cinnamon, and salt. Cut in butter until mixture resembles coarse crumbs. Sprinkle over top of blueberries. Bake until topping is light brown and blueberries are hot, about 30 minutes. Serve warm with ice cream or half-and-half.

Janet's Éclair Pudding

¾ box (1 lb.) of graham
   crackers
1 small package instant
   chocolate pudding
1 small package instant
   vanilla pudding
2 cups milk (divided)
2 cartons (8 oz. each) whipped
   topping

Frosting:
¼ cup margarine, melted
2 T. cocoa
powdered sugar

Line a 13 x 9-inch pan with graham crackers (leave whole). Set aside. In two separate bowls, mix chocolate and vanilla pudding with a little more than one cup milk each. Let puddings stand to thicken. Fold a carton of whipped topping into each bowl. Spoon chocolate pudding on top of crackers in pan, then top with an additional layer of crackers. Spoon vanilla pudding on top and add a final layer of crackers. Refrigerate for at least 1 hour.

For frosting, mix margarine and cocoa; add enough powdered sugar to make it spreadable. Spread over top layer of graham crackers.

Shiny Top Cobbler

5 cups berries
1½ T. lemon juice

Batter:
⅓ cup butter, softened
1½ cups sugar
1 cup milk
2 cups flour

2 tsp. baking powder
½ tsp. salt

Topping:
1½ cups sugar
½ tsp. salt
2 T. cornstarch
1½ cups boiling water

Spread berries in a 13 x 9-inch baking pan and sprinkle with lemon juice. For batter, cream butter and sugar. Whisk in milk, then stir in flour, baking powder, and salt. Beat until smooth, then spoon over fruit. For topping, mix sugar, salt, and cornstarch and sprinkle over batter. Pour boiling water over all. Bake at 350° for 1 hour.

Lemon Delight

If you want a place in the sun, you will have to expect some blisters.

Crust:
2 cups flour
1 cup butter, softened
½ cup chopped pecans

First Layer:
2 packages (8 oz. each) cream cheese

2 cups powdered sugar
2 cartons (8 oz. each) whipped topping, divided

Second Layer:
5 cups milk
3 packages lemon instant pudding

Mix crust ingredients and press into a 13 x 9-inch pan. Bake at 375° for 10–20 minutes or until light brown. Cool.

Mix cream cheese and powdered sugar. Fold in 2 cups whipped topping. Spread on crust. Whisk milk and pudding. Spread on top of cream cheese layer. Spoon remaining whipped topping over lemon layer. Refrigerate until ready to serve.

Strawberry Pretzel Dessert

2 cups crushed pretzels (about 8 oz.)

¾ cup butter, melted

3 T. sugar

Filling:

2 cups whipped topping

1 package (8 oz.) cream cheese, softened

1 cup sugar

Topping:

1 package (6 oz.) strawberry gelatin

2 cups boiling water

2 packages (16 oz. each) frozen sliced strawberries with syrup, thawed

additional whipped topping, optional

Combine pretzels, melted butter, and sugar. Press into the bottom of an ungreased 13 x 9-inch baking pan. Bake at 350° for 10 minutes. Cool. For filling, beat the whipped topping, cream cheese, and sugar until smooth. Spread over crust and chill at least 30 minutes. For topping, dissolve the gelatin in boiling water. Stir in the strawberries with syrup; refrigerate until partially set. Carefully spoon over filling. Refrigerate until firm (4–6 hours). Cut into squares; serve with additional whipped topping if desired.

Those who deserve love the least need it the most.

Apple Dumplings

2½ cups water

1¼ cups sugar

½ tsp. cinnamon

¼ cup plus 2 T. butter, divided

2 cups flour

2 tsp. baking powder

1 tsp. salt

¾ cup shortening

½ cup milk

6 small tart apples, peeled and cored

cinnamon-sugar

additional milk

In a small saucepan, combine the water, sugar, and cinnamon. Cook and stir over medium heat until sugar is dissolved, about 5 minutes. Add ¼ cup butter; stir until melted. Remove from the heat and set aside. Combine the flour, baking powder, and salt in medium bowl. Cut in the shortening until the mixture resembles coarse crumbs. Stir in milk. Divide pastry into 6 portions. On a lightly floured surface, roll each portion into a 6-inch square. Place an apple in the center of each. Sprinkle with cinnamon-sugar and dot with remaining butter. Bring corners of pastry to center. Brush edges with milk; pinch edges to seal. Place in a greased 13 x 9-inch dish and drizzle with the reserved syrup. Bake uncovered at 375° for 35–40 minutes or until golden.

Mixed Fruit Cobbler

3 pears, peeled, cored, and
    sliced
2 large nectarines, peeled,
    pitted, and sliced
2 large peaches, peeled,
    pitted, and sliced
⅓ cup sugar
2 T. cornstarch
1 T. cold butter, cut into
    small pieces

Topping:
1 cup flour
½ cup yellow cornmeal
⅓ cup sugar
2 tsp. baking powder
¼ tsp. cinnamon
⅛ tsp. salt
½ cup milk
¼ cup vegetable oil

Place all fruit in large bowl. Mix together sugar and cornstarch and sprinkle over fruit. Toss gently to combine and spoon into greased 8-inch square dish. Dot with butter.

For topping, mix dry ingredients. Add milk and oil until dry ingredients are just moistened. Spread evenly over filling. Bake at 375° for 35–40 minutes.

Note: The fruit should be ripe.

Rhubarb Crumble

8 cups chopped fresh or
  frozen rhubarb
1¼ cups sugar, divided
2½ cups flour
½ cup brown sugar
¼ cup quick-cooking oats
1 cup cold butter

Custard Sauce:
6 egg yolks
½ cup sugar
2 cups whipping cream
1¼ tsp. vanilla extract

In a saucepan, combine rhubarb and ¾ cup sugar. Cover and cook over medium heat, stirring occasionally, until the rhubarb is tender, about 10 minutes. Pour into a greased 13 x 9-inch pan. Combine flour, brown sugar, oats, and remaining ½ cup sugar. Cut in butter until crumbly and sprinkle mixture over rhubarb. Bake at 400° for 30 minutes. Meanwhile, in a saucepan, whisk the egg yolks and sugar together. Stir in cream. Cook and stir over low heat until thermometer reads 160° and mixture thickens, about 15–20 minutes. Remove from heat and stir in vanilla. Serve warm over rhubarb crumble.

Note: The rhubarb in this recipe is pretty sour. Add more sugar to rhubarb if desired.

*If we growl
all day we're
likely to feel
dog tired
at night.*

Peachy Cream Dessert

1 cup cold butter
2 cups self-rising flour
1 cup chopped pecans
1 8-oz. package cream cheese,
  softened
2 cups powdered sugar

1 carton (8 oz.) whipped
  topping
5 peaches, peeled and thinly
  sliced
1 container (14 oz.) peach
  glaze

Cut butter into flour until crumbly; stir in pecans. Press into a greased 13 x 9-inch baking dish. Bake at 350° for 25 minutes or until lightly browned. Cool.

Beat cream cheese and powdered sugar until fluffy. Beat in whipped topping and spread over cooled crust. Arrange peaches over cream cheese layer. Carefully spread glaze over peaches. Refrigerate until ready to serve.

Amish Vanilla Ice Cream

2 cups light corn syrup
8 T. cornstarch
3 cups brown sugar
1 tsp. salt

12 cups milk
8 eggs, slightly beaten
3 T. vanilla
4 cups light cream

Combine corn syrup, cornstarch, brown sugar, salt, milk, and eggs in large saucepan and heat on low, stirring occasionally, until slightly thickened. Pour into ice cream freezer can and cool in refrigerator. Add vanilla and cream. Freeze in ice cream freezer according to manufacturer's directions.

Pumpkin Torte

Crust:
½ cup butter
1 cup flour
½ cup chopped pecans

Second Layer:
1 8-oz. package cream cheese
1½–2 cups powdered sugar
1 cup whipped topping

Third Layer:
1 packet unflavored gelatin
¼ cup cold water
½ cup brown sugar

¾ cup pumpkin
2 egg yolks
⅓ cup milk
¼ tsp. salt
¼ tsp. ginger
¼ tsp. cinnamon
¼ tsp. nutmeg
2 egg whites
scant ⅓ cup sugar
¼ tsp. cream of tartar

Fourth Layer:
whipped topping

Don't call the world dirty because you've forgotten to clean your windows.

For crust, combine butter, flour, and pecans. Press into a
13 x 9-inch pan and bake at 350° for 15 minutes. Let cool.
Beat together cream cheese and powdered sugar until fluffy.
Gently fold in whipped topping. Spread onto cooled crust and
refrigerate. For third layer, dissolve gelatin in water and set aside.
In saucepan, bring brown sugar, pumpkin, egg yolks, milk, salt,
and spices to a boil. Remove from heat and add gelatin. Let cool.
In separate bowl, beat egg whites with sugar and cream of tartar
until stiff peaks form. Fold into cooled pumpkin mixture and
spread on top of cream cheese layer. Refrigerate. Spread whipped
topping on top just before serving.

Apricot Rice Custard

1 cup uncooked long grain
   rice
3 cups milk
½ cup sugar
½ tsp. salt
2 eggs, lightly beaten
½ tsp. vanilla extract
¼ tsp. almond extract
dash cinnamon

Sauce:
1 can (8½ oz.) apricot halves
1 can (8 oz.) crushed
   pineapple, undrained
⅓ cup brown sugar
2 T. lemon juice
1 T. cornstarch

A man is never old until his regrets outnumber his dreams.

Cook rice according to package directions. Stir in milk, sugar, and salt; bring to a boil. Reduce heat to low. Stir ½ cup of rice mixture into eggs; return all to pan. Cook and stir for 15 minutes or until mixture coats spoon (do not boil). Remove from heat; stir in extracts and cinnamon. Set aside.

For sauce, drain apricot syrup into saucepan. Chop apricots, add to syrup. Stir in remaining sauce ingredients and bring to a boil. Boil for 2 minutes, stirring occasionally. Serve sauce and custard warm or chilled.

Aunt Rose's Coffee Ice Cream

2 T. unflavored gelatin
3 cups milk, divided
2 cups sugar
¼ tsp. salt
6 eggs

1½ quarts light cream
1 package vanilla instant
   pudding
1 tsp. vanilla
2 T. instant coffee

In large bowl, soften gelatin in ½ cup cold milk. Scald 1½ cups milk and stir into gelatin mixture until it dissolves. Add sugar and salt, stirring until dissolved. Add remaining 1 cup milk and set aside. Beat eggs for 5 minutes on high. Add light cream, pudding, vanilla, and coffee. Fold in gelatin mixture. Chill in refrigerator for an hour, then freeze in ice cream freezer according to manufacturer's directions.

Cream Puff Dessert

1 cup water
½ cup butter
1 cup flour
4 eggs

Filling:
1 8-oz. package cream cheese
3½ cups cold milk
2 packages (3.9 oz. each)
    instant chocolate
    pudding mix

Topping:
1 carton (8 oz.) whipped
    topping
¼ cup milk chocolate ice
    cream topping
¼ cup caramel ice cream
    topping
⅓ cup chopped almonds

Many a little squirt thinks he's a fountain of wisdom.

In a saucepan over medium heat, bring water and butter to a boil. Add flour all at once and stir until a smooth ball forms. Remove from the heat and let stand for 5 minutes. Add the eggs, one at a time, beating well after each addition. Beat until smooth. Spread into a greased 13 x 9-inch pan. Bake at 400° for 30–35 minutes or until puffed and golden brown. Cool.

Meanwhile, in a mixing bowl, beat cream cheese, milk, and pudding mix until smooth. Spread over cooled puff and refrigerate for 20 minutes. Spread with whipped topping and refrigerate. Just before serving, drizzle with chocolate and caramel toppings; sprinkle with almonds. Yield: 12 servings.

Mr. Brunson's Butter Pecan Ice Cream

From *A Baby for Hannah*

"That sounds good to me," Mr. Brunson said. "What better time to speak of love than over cherry pie and butter pecan ice cream?"

6 large egg yolks	¼ tsp. salt
2 cups heavy cream	2 cups whole milk
6 T. butter	1 tsp. vanilla
1 cup brown sugar	1 cup pecans

In a medium sized heat-safe bowl, whisk together the egg yolks until well blended. Set aside. Pour the cream into a metal bowl set in a larger bowl of ice and set a medium-mesh sieve on top. Set aside. In a medium thick-bottomed saucepan on medium heat, melt the butter and cook, stirring constantly, until it just begins to brown. Add the brown sugar and salt. Stir until the sugar completely melts. Slowly add the milk, stirring to incorporate. It will foam up initially, so make sure you are using a pan with high enough sides. Heat until all of the sugar is completely dissolved. Do not let boil or the mixture may curdle.

Whisk in hand, slowly pour half of the milk and sugar mixture into the eggs, whisking constantly to incorporate. Then add the warmed egg mixture back into the saucepan with the remaining milk-sugar mixture. Stir the mixture constantly over medium heat with a wooden or heatproof rubber spatula, scraping the bottom as you stir, until the mixture thickens and coats the spatula, about 5–7 minutes. Pour the custard through the sieve and stir it into the cream. Add vanilla and stir until cool over the ice bath. Chill mixture thoroughly in the refrigerator.

While the mixture is chilling, preheat the oven to 350°. Lay out the pecans on a roasting pan in a single layer. Bake for 6 minutes until lightly toasted. Let cool. Once cool, roughly chop the pecans and set aside. Note: If you want an extra punch to this ice cream, brush the pecans with melted butter and sprinkle with salt before roasting.

Once the ice cream mixture is thoroughly chilled, freeze in your ice cream maker according to the manufacturer's instructions. Once the ice cream has been formed in the ice cream maker, it will be fairly soft. Fold in the chopped pecans. Scoop into an airtight plastic container and place in the freezer for at least an hour, preferably several hours. If it has been frozen for more than a day, you may need to let it sit at room temperature for a few minutes to soften it before serving.

Yield: 1½ quarts.

The best gifts are wrapped in heart-strings.

The Amish bishop was sitting on his front porch
late on a Saturday afternoon when a buggy
came into the lane. With a sigh, he listened to
the man's complaint against a particular church
member, nodding slowly. "Yah, yah," he said.
"I'm glad you understand the problem," the man
said, leaving in a rattling of buggy wheels.
Moments later, another buggy raced in the lane, and
tied up at the hitching post. The accused church member
marched to the porch, and gave his version of events.
"Yah, yah," the bishop said.
"I thought you'd understand," the man replied,
leaving with a big smile on his face.
The bishop had barely settled back into this rocker,
when his wife came out on the porch. "I heard all of
that," she told him. "If that's how you deal with your
church problems, no wonder nothing ever gets done."
"Yah, yah," the bishop agreed.

GRILLING

Yost Miller was subpoenaed to testify in
court on the accident he had witnessed.
"Can you tell the court what kind of vehicle the
defendant was driving?" the lawyer asked.
"No," Yost said.
"Surely you can tell whether the vehicle
was a Buick or a Cadillac," the lawyer
insisted. "Can't you tell one make of
car apart from another one?"
"No, I can't," Yost said. "Can you tell the
difference between a Holmes County buggy
and a Lancaster County buggy?"

Grilling Tips for Steak

Choose well-marbled cuts. The rib-eye is a favorite.

Brush the steak directly with oil before seasoning instead of oiling your grate.

If steak has a large amount of fat around the outside, make cuts in 2-inch intervals just through the outer layer. Make sure not to cut into the meat.

Finally let your steak rest, uncovered, after grilling for at least 5 minutes to redistribute the juices.

Any person who always feels sorry for himself, should be.

Cooking Times for Steaks

¾ inch - 4 minutes on each side

1 inch - 6 minutes on each side

1½ inches - 8 minutes on each side

This is for medium well, so for well-done 1 minute more on each side and for medium and medium rare, 1 and 2 minutes less on each side.

The Perfect Amish Steak

1 rib-eye steak
1 tsp. olive oil

½ tsp. kosher salt
½ tsp. coarsely ground pepper

Prepare grill for high heat. Brush steak evenly with oil; season with salt and pepper. Let steak stand at room temperature 30 minutes. Grill, covered with grill lid, over direct heat to desired doneness (see chart on page 117). Remove from grill and let stand, uncovered, 5 minutes before serving.

*People
are lonely
because they
build walls
instead of
bridges.*

Ruth's Grilled Fish

1 stick butter, melted
2 T. salt
½ tsp. garlic powder
1 cup water

⅔ cup apple juice
1 cup cider vinegar
4 lbs. whitefish fillets

Combine butter, salt, garlic powder, water, apple juice, and cider vinegar in saucepan. Bring to a boil and cook until reduced to 2 cups. Remove from heat and set aside.

Prepare grill for medium-high heat. Cover grill rack with heavy foil and poke holes into foil. Spray with cooking spray and set fillets on foil. Sop with sauce at least four times while grilling. Fish are done when flaky and tender (12–20 minutes).

BBQ Bacon Burgers

¼ cup mayonnaise
¼ cup barbecue sauce
4 bacon strips, cooked and
    crumbled
1½ tsp. dried minced onion
1½ tsp. steak seasoning

1 lb. ground beef
4 slices Swiss cheese
4 hamburger buns
lettuce leaves and tomato
    slices

In a small bowl, combine the mayonnaise and barbecue sauce. In another bowl, combine bacon, 2 tablespoons mayonnaise mixture, dried onion, and steak seasoning; crumble the beef over mixture and mix well. Shape into 4 patties. Grill burgers, covered, over medium heat for 5–7 minutes. Top with cheese. Cover and cook 1–2 minutes longer or until cheese is melted. Spread remaining mayonnaise mixture over buns; top each with a burger, lettuce, and tomato.

The cost of a thing is the amount of life which must be exchanged for it.

Lemon Grilled Chicken

1 lemon
2 T. olive oil
1 clove garlic, crushed
1 T. chopped fresh parsley
¼ tsp. thyme

¼ tsp. marjoram
¼ tsp. salt
¼ tsp. black pepper
4 skinless, boneless chicken
    breasts (about 6 oz. each)

Grate side of lemon to make 1 tablespoon of zest. Squeeze juice from the lemon into a bowl. Add zest, oil, garlic, parsley, thyme, marjoram, salt, and pepper. Add the chicken breasts and spoon the marinade over the chicken. Cover and chill for 30 minutes.

Preheat the grill to medium heat. Put the chicken pieces on the grill, reserving marinade. Cook chicken until cooked through, about 10 minutes on each side. Brush with reserved marinade 2–3 times during cooking. Serve immediately.

Barbecued Chicken

2 broiler/fryer chickens
    (2–3 lbs. each), cut up

Seasoning Mix:
3 T. salt
2 T. onion powder
1 T. paprika
2 tsp. garlic powder
1½ tsp. chili powder
1½ tsp. pepper
¼ tsp. turmeric
pinch red pepper

Sauce:
2 cups ketchup
3 T. brown sugar
2 T. dried minced onion
2 T. frozen orange juice
    concentrate, thawed
1 T. Seasoning Mix
½ tsp. liquid smoke

Pat chicken pieces dry so seasoning coats well; set aside. Combine seasoning mix ingredients. Reserve 1 tablespoon seasoning mix for sauce, sprinkle generously over both sides of the chicken. Grill chicken, skin side down, uncovered, over medium heat for 20 minutes. Turn; grill 20–30 minutes more or until chicken is tender and no longer pink. Meanwhile, combine all sauce ingredients. During last 10 minutes of grilling, brush chicken frequently with sauce. Yield: 12 servings.

Grilled Hamburgers

1½ lbs. hamburger
1 medium onion, chopped
¾ cup cubed soft bread
⅓ cup milk

¼ cup ketchup
1 T. prepared mustard
2 tsp. Worcestershire sauce
1½ tsp. salt

Mix all ingredients in large bowl. Form into patties and grill over medium-high heat to desired doneness.

Amish Rockets

½ lb. chicken breast strips
¾ cup Italian dressing, divided
4 oz. cream cheese, softened
⅛ tsp. salt

⅛ tsp. pepper
12 jalapeño peppers (about 3½ to 4 inches long)
12 thin bacon slices

Place chicken breast strips and ½ cup Italian dressing in a shallow dish or resealable plastic bag; cover or seal; chill 30 minutes. Remove chicken from marinade, discarding marinade. Grill chicken, covered with grill lid, over medium heat (300°–350°) 4–5 minutes on each side or until done, basting with remaining ¼ cup Italian dressing. Let chicken cool slightly and finely chop. Stir together chicken, cream cheese, salt, and pepper.

Cut peppers lengthwise down 1 side, leaving other side intact; remove seeds. Spoon 1½ to 2 tablespoons chicken mixture into cavity of each pepper. Wrap each pepper with 1 bacon slice, securing with 2 wooden toothpicks. This can all be done the day before serving. (For milder peppers look for jalapeño peppers with rounded tips.)

Grill stuffed jalapeños, without grill lid, over medium heat, 20–25 minutes or until bacon is crisp, turning frequently.

Reputation is man's opinion; character is God's.

Maple Glazed Chicken Wings

2½ lbs. chicken wings, skinned
¾ cup real maple syrup
½ cup chili sauce
1 small onion, diced

2 T. Dijon mustard
2 tsp. Worcestershire sauce
¼ to ½ tsp. dried crushed red pepper

Cut off wing tips and discard. Cut wings in half at joint. Stir together syrup, chili sauce, onion, Dijon, Worcestershire sauce, and red pepper. Remove and reserve 1 cup syrup mixture; cover and chill until ready to use. Place chicken in a resealable plastic bag. Pour remaining syrup mixture over chicken, turning to coat. Seal and chill 4 hours, turning chicken occasionally. Remove chicken from marinade; discard marinade.

To grill, place chicken over medium-low heat (250°–300°) and cook for 30 minutes or until done, turning and basting occasionally with reserved 1 cup mixture.

To bake, place chicken in a 15 x 10-inch pan coated with cooking spray. Bake at 375° for 45 minutes or until done, turning and basting every 10 minutes with reserved 1 cup syrup.

Grilling Rubs

Barbecue Rub:
1 T. chili powder
2 tsp. salt
2 tsp. light brown sugar
1 tsp. black pepper
1 tsp. cumin
½ tsp. garlic powder
¼ tsp. ground red pepper

Seasoned Salt Rub:
¼ cup salt
½ tsp. onion powder
½ tsp. ground celery seeds
½ tsp. garlic powder

½ tsp. paprika
½ tsp. pepper
¼ tsp. dried rosemary
¼ tsp. ground sage
¼ tsp. dried dill weed

Southwestern Rub:
1 T. salt
2 tsp. garlic powder
2 tsp. chili powder
2 tsp. ground cumin
2 tsp. pepper
½ tsp. unsweetened cocoa

For each rub, mix the ingredients and store in an airtight container. To use, ¼ cup of any of these rubs will season 4 chicken breasts, steaks, large chops, 2 pork tenderloins, or 2 lbs. of shrimp. Using your fingers, rub your choice of mix into the meat to lock in the flavor and you'll be ready to grill.

Maple Spare Ribs

2 slabs pork spareribs (about 6 lbs.)
1 cup real maple syrup
⅓ cup soy sauce
2 tsp. garlic powder
3 T. sweet rice wine

Bring spareribs and water to cover to a boil in large Dutch oven. Reduce heat and simmer 30 minutes. Drain. Place ribs in a 13 x 9-inch baking dish. Stir together maple syrup, soy sauce, garlic powder, and rice wine; pour over ribs. Preheat grill to medium-high on one side and arrange ribs over unlit side, reserving sauce. Grill, covered with grill lid, 1 hour. Reposition rib slabs, placing slab closest to heat source away from heat, and moving other slab closer to heat. Grill, covered with lid, 1 additional hour or until meat is tender, basting twice with reserved sauce. Remove ribs from grill and let stand 10 minutes. Cut ribs, slicing between bones.

Chipotle Barbecue Sauce

1½ cups cider vinegar
1 cup ketchup
¾ cup firmly packed light brown sugar
¼ cup Worcestershire sauce
1 T. butter
1 canned chipotle pepper, seeded and finely chopped
1 tsp. Creole seasoning

Mix all ingredients in saucepan. Bring to a boil, then reduce heat and simmer, stirring occasionally, for 5–7 minutes or until sugar is dissolved.

A bachelor is a man who's too fast to be caught or too slow to be worth catching.

Barbecue Rub for Ribs

1 cup firmly packed dark
    brown sugar
½ cup granulated garlic
½ cup kosher salt
½ cup paprika
2 T. granulated onion

1 T. dry mustard
1 T. Creole seasoning
1 T. chili powder
1 T. ground red pepper
1 T. cumin
1 T. black pepper

Stir together all ingredients. Store in an airtight container.
Massage into meat, wrap tightly in plastic wrap, and chill up
to 8 hours before grilling. This rub can be used on other meats
besides ribs.

*To see new
lands you
can either
travel many
miles to
distant
worlds, or
begin each
day at home
with love in
your heart.*

Favorite Chicken Barbecue

2 broilers (2 to 2½ lbs. each)
    or 5 lbs. leg quarters
½ cup oil
salt and pepper

Sauce:
1 can (8 oz.) tomato sauce
½ cup water
¼ cup molasses

2 T. butter
2 T. vinegar
2 T. minced onion
1 T. Worcestershire sauce
2 tsp. dry mustard
1 tsp. salt
¼ tsp. pepper
¼ tsp. chili powder

Brush chicken with oil and season with salt and pepper.
Combine all sauce ingredients in saucepan; simmer mixture
15–20 minutes. Set aside. Place chicken bone-side down on grill.
Grill on low for 25 minutes. Turn and grill for another 30–35
minutes; brushing with sauce and turning occasionally till done.
Very good. I sometimes make a double batch of the sauce.

Campfire Potatoes

5 medium potatoes, peeled
and thinly sliced
1 small sweet onion, chopped
4 T. butter
¾ cup shredded Cheddar
cheese

2 T. parsley, chopped
1 T. Worcestershire sauce
salt and pepper to taste
½ cup chicken broth

Place the potatoes and onions on a large piece of heavy-duty foil
(about 20 x 20 inches). Dot with butter. Combine the cheese,
parsley, Worcestershire sauce, salt, and pepper. Sprinkle over
potatoes and add broth. Seal edges of foil well. Grill on medium-
low for approximately 40 minutes. Yield: 4–6 servings.

It takes both
rain and
sunshine
to make
the garden
grow.

Colorful Grilled Veggies

10 cherry tomatoes, halved
2 celery ribs, thinly sliced
1 medium green pepper, sliced
1 medium sweet red pepper,
sliced
1 cup sliced fresh mushrooms
1 T. cider vinegar

1 T. oil
1 tsp. lemon juice
1 garlic clove, minced
1 tsp. dried basil
½ tsp. salt
½ tsp. pepper

Divide the vegetables between 2 pieces of heavy-duty foil (about
18 x 18 inches). In a small bowl, combine vinegar, oil, lemon
juice, garlic, basil, salt, and pepper; drizzle over vegetables.
Fold foil around vegetables and seal tightly. Grill, covered, over
medium heat for 10–15 minutes or until the vegetables are crisp-
tender. Yield: 6 servings.

MAIN DISHES

A tourist stopped in at the farm where
old Elmer Yoder was busy pumping
water with his hand pump.
"Where's route forty?" the tourist asked.
Elmer ignored him, continuing
to draw water.
"Where's route forty?" the
tourist now shouted.
Old Elmer continued filling his bucket.
"Are you ignorant or deaf?"
the tourist shouted next.
"Both," Elmer said, finally turning
around. "But at least I'm not lost."

Mexican Casserole

1½ lbs. ground beef
1 envelope taco seasoning
¾ cup water
1 can (16 oz.) refried beans
½ cup salsa
6 flour tortillas (6 inches)

2 cups frozen corn, thawed
2 cups (8 oz.) shredded
  Cheddar cheese
shredded lettuce, chopped
  tomatoes, sliced ripe
  olives, and sour cream

Cook beef until no longer pink; drain. Stir in taco seasoning and water. Bring to a boil. Reduce heat and simmer, uncovered, for 5 minutes. Meanwhile, in a microwave-safe bowl, combine beans and salsa. Cover and microwave for 1 or 2 minutes until spreadable. Place 3 tortillas in a greased round casserole dish. Layer with half of the beef, bean mixture, corn, and cheese; repeat layers. Bake uncovered, at 350° for 40–45 minutes or until cheese is melted. Let stand for 5 minutes. Serve with lettuce, tomatoes, olives, and sour cream to garnish.

Creamy Chicken Enchiladas

1 8-oz. package cream cheese,
  softened
2 T. water
2 tsp. onion powder
2 tsp. cumin
½ tsp. salt
¼ tsp. pepper
5 cups diced cooked chicken

20 flour tortillas (6 inches)
2 cans cream of chicken soup
2 cups sour cream
1 cup milk
2 cans (4 oz. each) chopped
  green chilies
2 cups (8 oz.) shredded
  Cheddar cheese

Beat cream cheese, water, onion powder, cumin, salt, and pepper until smooth. Stir in chicken. Place ¼ cup of this mixture down the center of each tortilla. Roll up and place seam-side down in two greased 13 x 9-inch pans. Combine soup, sour cream, milk, and chilies. Pour over enchiladas. Bake uncovered at 350° for 30–40 minutes. Sprinkle with cheese; bake 5 minutes longer or until cheese is melted.

Ella's Beef Casserole

From *A Wedding Quilt for Ella*

"It's boiling," she said, pulling her casserole out to wrap in the quilt again.

Walking over to the table, she set it down and headed out to the buggies again. By noon they were almost ready, and a portable dinner bell was rung loudly. The men lined up at the washbasins, scrubbing their hands and splashing water on their faces. They dried their hands on towels draped over chairs.

3 T. flour
1 tsp. salt
½ tsp. pepper
2 lbs. boneless round steak, cut into ½ inch cubes
2 T. oil
1 cup water
½ cup beef broth
1 minced garlic clove
1 T. dried minced onion

½ tsp. dried thyme
¼ tsp. dried rosemary, crushed
2 cups sliced fresh mushrooms
2 cups frozen peas, thawed
3 cups mashed potatoes (mashed with milk and butter)
1 T. melted butter
paprika

In a large resealable bag, combine flour, salt, and pepper; add beef cubes and shake to coat. In a skillet, brown beef in oil. Place beef and drippings in a greased shallow baking dish. To skillet, add water, broth, garlic, onion, thyme, and rosemary; bring to a boil. Simmer, uncovered, for 5 minutes; stir in mushrooms. Pour over meat; mix well. Cover and bake at 350° for 1½ to 1¾ hours or until beef is tender. Sprinkle peas over meat. Spread potatoes evenly over top. Brush with butter; sprinkle with paprika. Bake 15–20 minutes more. Yield: 6–8 servings.

Chicken and Dumpling Casserole

½ cup chopped onion
½ cup chopped celery
2 garlic cloves, minced
¼ cup butter
½ cup flour
2 tsp. sugar
1 tsp. salt

½ tsp. pepper
4 cups chicken broth
1 package (10 oz.) frozen peas
4 cups cubed cooked chicken

Dumplings:
2 cups buttermilk biscuit mix
⅔ cup milk

Sauté onion, celery, and garlic in butter until tender. Add flour, sugar, salt, pepper, and broth; bring to a boil. Cook and stir for 1 minute; reduce heat. Add peas and cook for 5 minutes, stirring. Stir in chicken. Pour into a greased 13 x 9-inch pan. For dumplings, combine biscuit mix and milk with fork until moistened. Drop by spoonfuls onto casserole making 12 dumplings. Bake, uncovered, at 350° for 30 minutes. Cover with foil and bake 10 minutes more.

The man who rows the boat seldom has time to rock it.

Lasagna

1½ lb. ground hamburger
1 clove garlic, minced
1 T. parsley flakes
1 lb. can diced tomatoes
2 6-oz. cans tomato paste
1½ cups water
3½ tsp. salt, divided
1 T. dried basil
1 package lasagna noodles,
    cooked according to
    package directions and
    rinsed in cold water

3 cups cottage cheese
½ tsp. pepper
2 beaten eggs
2 T. parsley flakes
½ cup Parmesan cheese
1 lb. mozzarella cheese

Brown hamburger; drain and set aside. In saucepan combine garlic, parsley, diced tomatoes, tomato paste, water, 1½ teaspoons salt, and basil. Let simmer on medium-low until thickened, about 30 minutes. Add meat to thickened sauce. Meanwhile, combine cottage cheese, pepper, eggs, remaining 2 teaspoons salt, parsley flakes, and Parmesan cheese. Place ½ of the cooked noodles on bottom of lasagna pan. Spoon over a layer of half the cottage cheese mixture, half the mozzarella, and half the meat sauce. Repeat layers, ending with mozzarella. Bake at 375° for 30 minutes. Let stand 15 minutes, then cut into servings. (This is best if prepared the night before and refrigerated till the next day, then baked.)

If you think you have influence, try ordering some else's dog around.

Pork Chop Casserole

¾ cup flour
½ tsp. pepper
1 tsp. salt
6 pork chops (¾ to 1 inch thick)
2 T. vegetable oil
1 can (10¾ oz.) cream of mushroom soup

⅔ cup chicken broth
½ tsp. ground ginger
¼ tsp. dried rosemary, crushed
1 cup (8 oz.) sour cream, divided
1 (2.8 oz.) can of French-fried onions, divided

Combine flour, pepper, and salt; dredge pork chops. Heat oil in large skillet and fry pork chops until browned. Place in a single layer in an ungreased 13 x 9-inch pan. Combine soup, broth, ginger, rosemary, and ½ cup sour cream; pour over chops. Sprinkle with half of the onions. Cover and bake at 350° for 45–50 minutes. Stir remaining sour cream into sauce. Top chops with remaining onions. Return to the oven, uncovered, for 10 minutes. Yield: 6 servings.

Chicken Casserole

8 slices of bread (crust removed)
4 cups of cooked chicken, shredded
4 eggs, well beaten
¼ cup butter melted
½ cup mayonnaise

1 cup milk
1 cup chicken broth
1 tsp. salt
8 slices of cheese
2 cans cream of celery soup
Buttered bread crumbs

Place bread on bottom of greased casserole dish. Put chicken on top of bread. Mix eggs, butter, mayonnaise, milk, broth, and salt. Pour over chicken. Top with cheese slices. Pour soup over top. Sprinkle with buttered bread crumbs. Bake at 350° for 1¼ hour. (May be made evening before.)

Joy and Pain are friends. To find the one is to hold hands with the other.

Cordon Bleu Casserole

4 cups cubed cooked turkey
3 cups cubed fully cooked ham
1¼ cups shredded Cheddar cheese, divided
1 cup chopped onion
¼ cup butter plus 2 T. butter, divided

⅓ cup flour
2 cups half-and-half
1¼ tsp. dill weed, divided
⅛ tsp. ground nutmeg
⅛ tsp. ground mustard
1 cup dry bread crumbs
¼ cup chopped walnuts

Combine turkey, ham, and 1 cup cheese; set aside. Sauté onion in ¼ cup butter. Stir in flour to form a paste. Gradually add half-and-half, stirring constantly. Bring to a boil. Boil 1 minute or until thick. Add 1 teaspoon dill weed, nutmeg, and ground mustard. Pour over meat mixture and toss gently to combine. Spoon into greased 13 x 9-inch pan. Melt remaining

2 tablespoons butter and toss with bread crumbs and remaining
¼ teaspoon dill weed. Mix in remaining ¼ cup cheese and
walnuts. Sprinkle over casserole. Bake, uncovered, at 350° for 30
minutes or until heated through.

Baked Spaghetti

*May we
always
pluck the
thistles
and plant
flowers
where
flowers
will grow.*

1 cup chopped onion
1 cup chopped green pepper
1 T. butter
1 can (28 oz.) diced tomatoes,
    undrained
1 can (4 oz.) mushroom stems
    and pieces, drained and
    chopped
1 can (2¼ oz.) sliced ripe
    olives, drained
2 tsp. dried oregano
1 lb. ground beef, browned
    and drained

salt and garlic salt to taste
12 oz. spaghetti, cooked and
    drained
2 cups (8 oz.) shredded
    Cheddar cheese, divided
1 can (10¾ oz.) condensed
    cream of mushroom soup,
    undiluted
¼ cup water
¼ cup grated Parmesan
    cheese

In a large skillet, sauté onion and green pepper in butter until
tender. Add tomatoes, mushrooms, olives, oregano, ground beef,
salt, and garlic salt. Simmer uncovered for 10 minutes.

Place half of the spaghetti in a greased 13 x 9-inch baking dish.
Top with half the vegetable mixture and sprinkle with 1 cup
Cheddar cheese. Repeat layers. Mix the soup and water and pour
over casserole. Sprinkle with Parmesan cheese. Bake uncovered
at 350° for 30 minutes or until heated through. Yield: 12 servings

Note: This casserole can be assembled the day before and
refrigerated until ready to bake. If you do this, let it set out for a
while and then bake at 300° until heated through.

Enchilada Casserole

1 lb. ground beef
1 large onion, chopped
2 cups salsa
1 can (15 oz.) black beans,
    rinsed and drained
¼ cup Italian salad dressing
2 T. taco seasoning
¼ tsp. cumin

6 flour tortillas (8 inches)
¾ cup sour cream
1 cup (4 oz.) shredded
    Mexican cheese blend
1 cup shredded lettuce
1 medium tomato, chopped
¼ cup minced fresh cilantro

In a large skillet, cook beef and onion until meat is no longer pink, drain. Stir in salsa, beans, dressing, taco seasoning, and cumin. Place 3 tortillas in a greased 2-quart baking dish.

Layer with half of the meat mixture, sour cream, and cheese. Repeat layers. Cover and bake at 400° for 25 minutes. Uncover; bake 5–10 minutes longer or until heated through. Let stand for 5 minutes before topping with lettuce, tomato, and cilantro.

In nature there are neither rewards nor punishments. There are only consequences.

Enchiladas

1 lb. lean ground beef
1 large onion, chopped
¼ tsp. salt
1 small garlic clove, minced
2 cups (8 oz.) shredded
    Cheddar cheese
1 can (10¾ oz.) condensed
    cream of chicken soup,
    undiluted

1 package (8 oz.) Velveeta
    cheese, cubed
¾ cup evaporated milk
1 can (4 oz.) chopped green
    chilies, drained
1 jar (2 oz.) diced pimientos,
    drained
12 corn tortillas (6 inches)
¼ cup canola oil

In a large skillet, cook the beef, onion, and salt until meat is no longer pink. Add garlic; cook 1 minute longer. Drain. Stir in

Cheddar cheese; set aside. Meanwhile, in large saucepan, cook and stir the soup, Velveeta, and milk over medium heat until cheese is melted. Stir in chilies and pimientos. In a large skillet, fry tortillas, one at a time, in oil for 5 seconds on each side or until golden brown. Drain on paper towels. Place a scant ¼ cup of reserved meat mixture down center of each tortilla. Roll up and place seam side down in greased 13 x 9-inch baking dish. Pour cheese sauce on top. Cover and bake at 350° for 25–30 minutes or until heated through.

Reuben Casserole

Wise men are not always silent, but they know when to be.

5 cups uncooked egg noodles
2 cans (14 oz. each) sauerkraut, rinsed and drained
2 cans (10¾ oz. each) condensed cream of chicken soup
¾ cup milk

½ cup chopped onion
3 T. prepared mustard
¾ lb. sliced deli corned beef, chopped
2 cups (8 oz.) shredded Swiss cheese
2 slices day-old light rye bread
2 T. butter, melted

Cook noodles according to package directions. Meanwhile, in a large bowl, combine the sauerkraut, soup, milk, onion, and mustard. Drain noodles; stir into sauerkraut mixture. Transfer to a greased 13 x 9-inch baking dish and sprinkle with corned beef and cheese. Place bread in a food processor; cover and process until mixture resembles coarse crumbs. Toss crumbs with butter; sprinkle over casserole. Bake uncovered, at 350° for 40–45 minutes or until bubbly.

Sausage Lasagna

1 lb. ground beef
¾ lb. bulk pork sausage
3 cans (8 oz. each) tomato
   sauce
2 cans (6 oz. each) tomato
   paste
2 garlic cloves, minced
2 tsp. sugar
1 tsp. Italian seasoning
1 tsp. salt
½ tsp. pepper

3 eggs
3 T. minced fresh parsley
3 cups (24 oz.) 4% small-curd
   cottage cheese
1 carton (8 oz.) ricotta cheese
½ cup grated Parmesan
   cheese
9 lasagna noodles, cooked and
   drained
6 slices provolone cheese
3 cups (12 oz.) shredded
   mozzarella cheese, divided

In a large skillet, cook beef and sausage until no longer pink;
drain. Add the tomato sauce, tomato paste, garlic, sugar,
seasoning, salt, and pepper. Bring to a boil. Reduce heat; simmer,
uncovered, for 1 hour, stirring occasionally.

In a large bowl, combine eggs and parsley. Stir in the cottage
cheese, ricotta, and Parmesan cheese. Spread 1 cup meat sauce
in an ungreased 13 x 9-inch baking dish. Layer with three
noodles, provolone cheese, 2 cups cottage cheese mixture, and
1 cup mozzarella. Add another 3 noodles, 2 cups meat sauce,
remaining cottage cheese mixture, and 1 cup mozzarella. Top
with the remaining noodles, meat sauce, and mozzarella (dish
will be full). Cover and bake at 375° for 50 minutes. Uncover;
bake 20 minutes longer or until heated through. Let stand for 15
minutes before cutting.

Easiest Pot Roast Dinner

1 (3 to 4 lb.) boneless chuck roast or arm roast	1 lb. baby carrots
5 large russet potatoes, quartered	1 (1.25 oz.) package onion soup mix
2 celery stalks, cut in 2-inch pieces	1 (14 oz.) can whole peeled tomatoes, sliced in thirds and liquid reserved

It is not the ship in the water but the water in the ship that sinks it.

Preheat oven to 275°. Prepare a 15 x 10-inch baking dish by laying two 24-inch long pieces of heavy-duty aluminum foil crosswise in the dish. Lay roast in center and arrange potatoes, celery, and carrots around roast. Sprinkle onion soup mix over top of roast. Place tomatoes on top. Add water to reserved tomato liquid to fill can and pour over vegetables surrounding roast. Bring ends of foil together all around, creating a seal so that juices do not escape. Place dish in oven and roast for 8 hours. Transfer roast to serving platter, surround it with vegetables, and spoon pan juices over everything.

Note: To decrease cooking time, preheat oven to 325° and roast for 3 hours.

Sloppy Joe Bake

1 lb. ground beef	2 tsp. prepared mustard
1 cup chopped onion	1½ cups Bisquick
1 can (15 oz.) tomato sauce	1 cup milk
½ cup ketchup	2 eggs
⅓ cup brown sugar	

Preheat oven to 400°. In a large skillet, cook ground beef and onion until beef is no longer pink. Drain. Stir in tomato sauce, ketchup, brown sugar, and mustard. Heat to boiling. Spoon into ungreased 13 x 9-inch pan.

Stir Bisquick, milk, and eggs with fork until blended. Carefully pour over beef mixture. Bake 20 to 25 minutes or until light golden brown.

Chicken Veggie Fajitas

3 T. lemon juice
1 T. soy sauce
1 T. Worcestershire sauce
2 tsp. vegetable oil
1 garlic clove, minced
½ tsp. cumin
½ tsp. oregano
¾ lb. boneless, skinless chicken breasts, cut into ½-inch thick strips
1 small onion, sliced and separated into rings

½ each of medium red, green, and yellow peppers, julienned
4 6-inch flour tortillas, warmed

Toppings:
shredded Cheddar cheese
sour cream
taco sauce

Worry is interest paid on trouble before it is due.

In small bowl, combine the lemon juice, soy sauce, Worcestershire sauce, oil, garlic, cumin, and oregano. Place chicken, onion, and peppers in a single layer in a greased 15 x 10-inch pan. Drizzle with ¼ cup of the lemon juice mixture. Broil 4–6 inches from heat for 4 minutes. Turn chicken and vegetables and drizzle with remaining mixture. Broil 4 minutes longer or until chicken juices run clear. Serve on tortillas with toppings.

Chicken Pot Pie

Pastry:
1½ cups flour
1 tsp. salt
⅓ cup chilled butter, cut
    into pieces
1 large egg
2–3 T. ice water

Filling:
4 cups cubed cooked chicken
1 T. butter

1 lb. fresh mushrooms, sliced
¼ cup water
1½ cups whipping cream
2 T. flour
1½ tsp. or less paprika
½ tsp. salt
½ tsp. or less black pepper
¾ cup chicken broth

Egg Wash:
1 large egg, lightly beaten

For pastry, mix flour and salt. Cut butter into flour until coarse crumbs form. Beat together the egg and water. Add to flour mixture; mix lightly until soft dough forms. Shape into a disk, wrap in plastic wrap, and chill in the refrigerator for 1 hour.

For filling, place chicken in a 2-quart casserole. In large skillet, melt butter over low heat. Add mushrooms; increase the heat to medium-high; and sauté until browned and the liquid evaporates, about 5 minutes. Add the water; cook until almost evaporated, about 2 minutes. Add mushroom mixture to chicken; stir to combine.

In a medium saucepan, whisk together cream, flour, paprika, salt, and pepper; cook until thickened, about 5 minutes. Whisk in broth. Pour sauce over chicken mixture.

Preheat oven to 400°. On a lightly floured surface, roll out the pastry to fit the top of the casserole. Place on top of the filling. Trim and seal edges. Roll out trimmings. Cut out leaves and flowers. Brush pastry with egg wash; add decorations; brush again with egg wash. Bake until filling is bubbly and crust is browned, 25–30 minutes.

Dressing

1 cup celery, chopped
1 cup carrots, chopped
1 cup potatoes, chopped
½ cup onions, chopped
1 tsp. salt
water
1 quart chicken broth
1–2 cups cooked chicken,
    chopped
2 T. chicken flavored soup
    base or bouillon

1 loaf bread, toasted and
    cubed
4 eggs
3 cups milk
½ tsp. salt
¼ tsp. pepper
1 tsp. seasoned salt
1 tsp. parsley
½ cup butter, browned,
    divided

*One reason
a dog is such
a lovable
creature
is that his
tail wags
instead of
his tongue.*

Simmer vegetables in water to cover with 1 teaspoon salt until tender. Do not drain. Heat chicken broth with chicken and soup base to boiling. Pour over toasted bread cubes. Beat eggs, milk, seasonings, and half the browned butter and pour over bread. Toss gently to combine, then add vegetables. Drizzle remaining ¼ cup browned butter into roasting pan. Add dressing and bake at 350° for 1 hour or until done.

Chicken Rice Dinner

½ cup flour
1 tsp. salt
½ tsp. pepper
10 bone-in chicken thighs
    3 lbs.)
3 T. vegetable oil
1 cup uncooked rice

¼ cup chopped onion
2 garlic cloves, minced
1 can (4 oz.) mushroom stems
    and pieces, undrained
2 chicken bouillon cubes
2 cups boiling water

In a large bowl, combine flour, salt, and pepper; coat chicken pieces. In a large skillet, brown chicken in oil. Place rice in an ungreased 13 x 9-inch pan. Sprinkle with onion and garlic; top with mushrooms. Dissolve bouillon in boiling water; pour over all. Place chicken pieces on top. Cover and bake at 350° for 1 hour or until chicken juices run clear and rice is tender.

Underground Ham Casserole

He who strikes the first blow confesses that he has run out of ideas.

4 T. butter	1½ cups milk, divided
4 cups ham, cubed	2 cups shredded cheese
½ cup onions, chopped	4 quarts mashed potatoes
1 T. Worcestershire sauce	1 pint sour cream
2 cans cream of mushroom soup	½ cup milk

Melt butter; add ham, onions, and Worcestershire sauce. Fry until onions are tender. Transfer to roasting pan. In saucepan, heat soup, 1 cup milk, and cheese until cheese is melted. Pour over ham mixture. Mix potatoes, sour cream, and remaining ½ cup milk and spoon on top of cheese mixture. Bake at 325° until hot.

Variation: For the last layer, I will use my leftover mashed potatoes instead of the last 3 ingredients. Also, bacon bits may be sprinkled on last layer before baking.

Broccoli-Ham Hot Dish

2 packages (10 oz. each)
    frozen cut broccoli
2 cups cooked rice
6 T. butter
2 cups soft bread crumbs
    (about 2½ slices)
1 medium onion, chopped
3 T. flour

1 tsp. salt
¼ tsp. pepper
3 cups milk
1½ lbs. fully cooked ham,
    cubed
shredded Cheddar or Swiss
    cheese

Cook broccoli according to package directions; drain. Spoon rice into a 13 x 9-inch pan. Place broccoli over rice. Melt butter. Sprinkle 2 tablespoons of melted butter over the bread crumbs and set aside. In remaining butter, sauté onion until tender. Add flour, salt, and pepper, stirring constantly until bubbly. Stir in milk and continue cooking until sauce thickens and bubbles. Cook and stir for 1 minute; add ham and heat through. Pour over rice and broccoli. Sprinkle the bread crumbs over all. Bake at 350° for 30 minutes or until heated through. Sprinkle with cheese; let stand 5 minutes before serving. Yield: 8 servings.

The archer who overshoots his mark does no better than he who falls short of it.

Shipwreck

½ lb. sliced bacon
1 lb. ground beef
1 large onion, chopped

1 cup ketchup
½ cup brown sugar
1 can (32 oz.) pork and beans

In a skillet, cook bacon until crisp. Remove to paper towels to drain; crumble and set aside. Drain drippings from skillet. Brown the beef; drain. Add onion and cook until tender, about 5 minutes. Combine ketchup and brown sugar; stir into beef mixture. Stir in pork and beans and all but 2 tablespoons of the bacon. Transfer to an 8-inch square pan. Top with remaining bacon. Bake uncovered at 350° for 1 hour.

Chicken Fajitas

¼ cup lime juice
1 garlic clove, minced
1 tsp. chili powder
½ tsp. cumin
2 whole boneless skinless chicken breasts, cut into strips
1 medium onion, cut into thin wedges
½ medium sweet red pepper, cut into strips
½ medium yellow pepper, cut into strips
½ medium green pepper, cut into strips
½ cup salsa
12 flour tortillas (8 inches)
1½ cups (6 oz.) shredded Cheddar or Monterey Jack cheese

To admit I was wrong is but saying I am wiser today than I was yesterday.

Combine lime juice, garlic, chili powder, and cumin. Add chicken; stir. Marinate for 15 minutes. In a nonstick skillet, cook onion, chicken, and marinade for 3 minutes or until chicken is no longer pink. Add peppers; sauté for 3–5 minutes or until crisp-tender. Stir in salsa. Divide mixture among tortillas; top with cheese. Roll up and serve.

Spanish Rice and Chicken

1 broiler/fryer chicken (2½ to 3 lbs.), cut up
1 tsp. garlic salt
1 tsp. celery salt
1 tsp. paprika
1 cup uncooked rice
¾ cup chopped onion
¾ cup chopped green pepper
¼ cup minced fresh parsley
1½ cups chicken broth
1 cup chopped tomatoes
1½ tsp. salt
1½ tsp. chili powder

Place chicken in a greased 13 x 9-inch pan. Combine garlic salt, celery salt, and paprika; sprinkle over chicken. Bake uncovered at

425° for 20 minutes. Remove chicken from pan. Combine rice, onion, green pepper, and parsley; spoon into pan. In a saucepan, bring broth, tomatoes, salt, and chili powder to a boil. Pour over rice mixture; mix well. Place chicken pieces on top. Cover and bake for 45 minutes or until chicken and rice are tender. Yield: 4–6 servings.

Ham-Stuffed Manicotti

8 manicotti shells
½ cup chopped onion
1 T. vegetable oil
3 cups (1 lb.) ground fully cooked ham
1 can (4 oz.) sliced mushrooms, drained
1 cup (4 oz.) shredded Swiss cheese, divided

3 T. grated Parmesan cheese
¼ to ½ cup chopped green pepper
3 T. butter
3 T. flour
2 cups milk
paprika
chopped fresh parsley

A mistake is evidence that you have tried.

Cook manicotti according to package directions; set aside. Sauté onion in oil until tender. Remove from heat. Add ham, mushrooms, half of the Swiss cheese, and Parmesan; set aside. In a saucepan, sauté green pepper in butter until tender. Stir in flour until thoroughly combined. Add milk; cook, stirring constantly, until thickened and bubbly. Mix a quarter of the sauce into ham mixture. Stuff each shell with about ⅓ cup of filling. Place in a greased 11 x 7-inch baking dish. Top with remaining sauce; sprinkle with paprika. Cover and bake at 350° for 30 minutes or until heated through. Sprinkle with parsley and remaining Swiss cheese before serving.

Mexican Lasagna

1¼ lbs. ground beef
1 medium onion, chopped
4 cloves garlic, minced
2 cups salsa
1 can (16 oz.) refried beans
1 can (15 oz.) black beans,
    rinsed and drained
1 can (10 oz.) enchilada sauce
1 can (4 oz.) chopped green
    chilies

1 envelope taco seasoning
¼ tsp. pepper
6 flour tortillas (10 inches)
3 cups (12 oz.) shredded
    Mexican cheese blend,
    divided
2 cups crushed tortilla chips
sliced ripe olives, guacamole,
    chopped tomatoes, and
    sour cream, optional

*Better to
let them
wonder why
you didn't
speak than
to wonder
why you did.*

In a large skillet, cook beef and onion until meat is no longer pink. Add garlic; cook 1 minute longer. Drain. Stir in the salsa, beans, enchilada sauce, chilies, taco seasoning, and pepper; heat through. Spread 1 cup meat mixture in greased 13 x 9-inch baking dish. Layer with 2 tortillas, a third of the remaining meat mixture, and 1 cup cheese. Repeat layers. Top with remaining tortillas and meat mixture. Cover and bake at 375° for 30 minutes. Sprinkle with the remaining cheese and top with tortilla chips. Bake 10–15 minutes longer or until cheese is melted. Garnish with remaining ingredients.

Creamed Chicken and Biscuits

½ large onion, chopped
1½ tsp. butter, melted
4 cups chopped cooked
    chicken
1 can cream of chicken soup
1 cup sour cream

½ cup milk
½ cup chopped pimiento
1 cup shredded mild Cheddar
    cheese, divided
6 frozen biscuits, thawed

Sauté onion in butter until tender. Combine onion, chicken, soup, sour cream, milk, and pimiento and mix well. Spoon mixture into a greased 11 x 7-inch baking dish. Bake 15 minutes at 350°. Sprinkle with ¾ cup of the Cheddar cheese. Arrange biscuits over top. Sprinkle with remaining cheese. Bake until biscuits are golden brown and the sauce is bubbly, about 20 minutes.

Biscuit Pizza Bake

1 lb. ground beef
2 tubes (12 oz. each)
  refrigerated buttermilk
  biscuits
1 can (15 oz.) pizza sauce
1 cup chopped green pepper
½ cup chopped onion

1 can (4 oz.) mushroom stems
  and pieces, drained
1 package (3½ oz.) sliced
  pepperoni
1 cup (4 oz.) shredded
  mozzarella cheese
1 cup (4 oz.) shredded
  Cheddar cheese

Cook beef until no longer pink; drain. Quarter biscuits; place in a greased shallow 3-quart baking dish. Top with pizza sauce. Sprinkle beef over sauce. Layer with green pepper, onion, mushrooms, pepperoni, and cheeses. Bake, uncovered, at 350° for 25–30 minutes or until cheese is melted. Let stand 5–10 minutes before serving.

Spanish Rice with Venison

2 lbs. ground venison or beef
1 onion, chopped
1 green pepper, chopped
⅓ cup butter
1 can (28 oz.) stewed tomatoes
1 can (15 oz.) tomato sauce

1 cup water
1½ to 2 tsp. cumin
2½ tsp. chili powder
2 tsp. salt
2 tsp. Worcestershire sauce
1 cup or more of instant rice
    (white or brown)

Fry meat, onion, and green pepper in butter. Add the rest of the ingredients except rice. Simmer and taste for seasoning. Add rice and simmer until rice is done.

Baked Burritos

8 oz. sour cream
½ can cream of chicken soup
1 package taco seasoning
1 lb. ground beef, cooked
2 cups cooked rice

1 can refried beans
7–8 large flour tortillas, room
    temperature
8 oz. grated Cheddar cheese

Mix sour cream and soup. Spread just a little in 13 x 9-inch pan. Combine taco seasoning and meat. Put meat, rice, and beans on each tortilla. Fold and tuck ends under. Place in pan. Spread with remaining soup mixture. Sprinkle with cheese. Bake at 350° for 30–35 minutes. Serve with salsa or salad.

Chili Nacho Supper

2½ lbs. ground beef
3 15-oz. cans tomato sauce
2 16-oz. cans pinto beans,
  rinsed and drained
2 envelopes chili mix

2 lbs. American cheese, cubed
1 cup whipping cream
2 packages (16 oz. each) corn
  chips
sour cream

Cook beef and drain. Add tomato sauce, beans, and chili mix. Heat through. Add cheese and cream. Cook until cheese is melted. Serve over chips. Top with sour cream.

To handle yourself use your head, to work with others, use your heart.

Deep-Dish Pizza

Crust:
1 package yeast (2¼ tsp.)
1 cup warm water
1 tsp. sugar
1 tsp. salt
2 T. vegetable oil
2½ cups flour

Filling:
1 lb. hamburger
1 16-oz. can whole tomatoes,
  drained

1 T. instant minced onion
1 tsp. oregano
1¼ tsp. salt, divided
¼ tsp. pepper
⅛ tsp. garlic powder
1 small green pepper, cut into
  thin strips
1 4-oz. can mushroom stem
  and pieces, drained
1 cup (4 oz.) shredded
  mozzarella cheese

Cook hamburger until no longer pink; drain. Dissolve yeast in warm water. Stir in remaining crust ingredients; beat vigorously 20 strokes. Let rest 5 minutes. Mix tomatoes, onion, oregano, ¼ teaspoon salt, pepper, and garlic powder; break up tomatoes with fork.

Press dough evenly on bottom and halfway up sides of greased 13 x 9-inch pan. Sprinkle with hamburger. Sprinkle with remaining 1 teaspoon salt. Spoon sauce onto hamburger; top with green pepper, mushrooms, and cheese. Bake at 425° for 20–25 minutes or until cheese is light brown. Yield: 8 servings.

Taco Rice

The taller bamboo grows, the lower it bends.

1 lb. hamburger
1 onion, chopped
½ package taco seasoning
1 16-oz. can chunk tomatoes, drained (reserve juice)
1 cup rice
water

1 cup mayonnaise
1 cup sour cream
1 cup shredded Cheddar cheese
2 cups Bisquick mix
milk

Fry hamburger and onion until brown. Drain. Add taco seasoning and tomatoes. Cook rice with reserved tomato juice and enough water to make 2½ cups. When rice is soft, mix rice with hamburger mixture. Pour into 13 x 9-inch pan. Mix mayonnaise, sour cream, and shredded cheese and put on top of hamburger mixture. Make a thin batter of Bisquick and milk. Pour on top of cheese mixture. Bake at 400° for 30 minutes.

Pennsylvania Filled Pig Stomach

1 medium head cabbage,
 shredded
7 medium potatoes, diced
2 lbs. sausage, with or
 without skins

½ tsp. salt
¼ tsp. pepper
clean pig stomach

If using sausage with skins, slice to about ½-inch widths. Mix cabbage with potatoes, sausage, and seasonings. Fill pig stomach. Bake at 350° for 2½ hours.

Pork Chops Olé

6 loin pork chops (½ inch
 thick)
2 T. cooking oil
seasoned salt, salt, and pepper
 to taste
¾ cup uncooked long grain
 rice
1½ cups water

1 8-oz. can tomato sauce
½ envelope taco seasoning
 mix (about 2 T.)
1 medium green pepper,
 chopped
½ cup shredded Cheddar
 cheese

In a large skillet, brown pork chops in oil; sprinkle with seasoned salt, salt, and pepper.

Meanwhile, in a greased 13 x 9-inch pan, combine rice, water, tomato sauce, and taco seasoning; mix well. Arrange chops over rice; top with green pepper. Cover and bake at 350° for 1½ hours. Uncover and sprinkle with cheese; return to the oven until cheese is melted. Yield: 4–6 servings.

Chicken Tortilla Pie

3 T. vegetable oil
1 medium onion, sliced
1 large clove garlic, minced
1 T. chili powder
1 tsp. cumin
¼ tsp. black pepper
1 cup canned crushed
   tomatoes

vegetable oil for frying
6 corn tortillas (6-inch size)
½ cup sour cream
2 cups shredded Monterey
   Jack cheese (8 oz.)
2 cups shredded cooked
   chicken
6 canned whole green chilies,
   split lengthwise

The steam
that blows
the whistle
can't be
used to turn
the wheels.

Heat 1 tablespoon oil; add onion, garlic, chili powder, cumin, and pepper. Cook, stirring frequently, 5 minutes. In a blender, combine onion mixture and tomatoes; blend until smooth, 1 minute. In the same skillet, heat remaining 2 tablespoons oil; stir in tomato mixture, cook, stirring constantly, until sauce thickens, 5 minutes. Transfer to bowl.

Wipe skillet clean with paper towels. Pour enough oil in to reach ¼ inch depth. Heat oil over high heat. Add tortillas, one at a time, and cook until golden, 2–3 seconds on a side. Transfer tortillas to paper towels to drain.

To assemble, place 2 tortillas in a 9 x 6-inch baking dish. Spread with ¼ each of the sauce, sour cream, cheese, and 1 cup chicken. Lay 3 chili slices flat on top of chicken. Top with 2 more tortillas. Repeat to make another layer. Top with remaining tortillas, sauce, sour cream, and cheese. Cover with aluminum foil. Bake at 350° for 30 minutes.

Meatballs in Mushroom Gravy

2 tsp. salt
8 soda crackers, crushed
1½ lb. ground beef
2 eggs
¼ cup chopped celery

¼ cup milk
¼ cup chopped onion
¼ tsp. pepper
1 can cream of mushroom
  soup
1 can water

Mix all ingredients except soup and water. Shape into balls; brown in oil. Put in roaster or casserole dish. Mix soup and water and pour over meatballs. Bake at 350° for 30 minutes.

Be what you wish others to become.

Barbecued Meatballs

3 lbs. ground beef
1 12-oz. can evaporated milk
1 cup oatmeal
1 cup cracker crumbs
2 eggs
½ tsp. garlic powder
2 tsp. salt

½ tsp. pepper
2 tsp. chili powder
Sauce:
2 cups ketchup
1 cup brown sugar
½ tsp. liquid smoke
¼ cup chopped onion

Mix all ingredients for meatballs; shape into walnut-sized balls. Place meatballs in a single layer on wax paper-lined cookie sheets; freeze until solid. Store frozen meatballs in freezer bags until ready to cook. For sauce, mix all ingredients until sugar is dissolved. Place frozen meatballs in a 13 x 9-inch pan. Pour sauce over meatballs. Bake at 350° for 1 hour. Yields about 80 meatballs.

Venison Meatloaf

2 eggs lightly beaten
1 8-oz. can tomato sauce
1 medium onion, chopped
1 cup dry bread crumbs
1½ tsp. salt
⅛ tsp. pepper

1½ lbs. ground venison

Glaze:
2 T. brown sugar
2 T. spicy brown mustard
2 T. white vinegar

Mix first 6 ingredients; add venison and mix well. Press into a 9 x 5-inch loaf pan. Combine glaze ingredients; pour over meatloaf. Bake uncovered at 350° for 70 minutes.

Tangy Meatballs

2 eggs, beaten
2 cups quick oats
1 cup chopped onion
2 tsp. salt
½ tsp. garlic powder
½ tsp. pepper
1 12-oz. can evaporated milk

3 lbs. lean ground beef

Sauce:
2 cups ketchup
1½ cups brown sugar
½ cup chopped onion
1–2 tsp. liquid smoke
½ tsp. garlic powder

Mix first seven ingredients. Add ground beef; mix well. Shape into 1½-inch balls and place in two 13 x 9-inch pans. Bake uncovered at 375° for 30 minutes. Remove from oven and drain. Place all of meatballs into one of the pans. For sauce, mix together sauce ingredients and bring to a boil. Pour over meatballs. Bake 20 additional minutes or until meatballs are done. Yield: 4 dozen.

Venison Meatballs

1 medium onion, finely
    chopped
½ cup uncooked instant rice
1 tsp. salt
¼ tsp. pepper
1 lb. ground venison
¼ lb. bacon, ground

¾ cup water
⅓ cup brown sugar
⅓ cup ketchup
⅓ cup condensed tomato
    soup
1 T. ground mustard
2 tsp. paprika

Combine the first four ingredients. Mix in venison and bacon.
Mix well. Shape into 1½-inch balls. Place in greased baking dish.
Combine remaining ingredients; pour over meatballs. Bake,
uncovered, at 375° for 35–45 minutes.

Note: You can make these ahead and refrigerate until ready to
bake. These are a favorite.

*Worse than
failure is
the failure
to try.*

Oven-Barbecued Chicken

cooking oil
3 to 4 lbs. chicken pieces
3 T. butter
⅓ cup onion, chopped
¾ cup ketchup
⅓ cup vinegar

3 T. brown sugar
½ cup water
2 tsp. prepared mustard
1 T. Worcestershire sauce
¼ tsp. salt
⅛ tsp. pepper

Fry chicken in oil until browned; drain. Place chicken in a 13 x
9-inch pan. In a saucepan, sauté onion in butter until tender; stir
in remaining ingredients. Simmer, uncovered, for 15 minutes.
Pour over chicken. Bake at 350° about 1 hour or until chicken is
done, basting occasionally. Yield: 6–8 servings.

Stuffed Chicken Rolls

6 large boneless, skinless chicken breast halves
6 slices fully cooked ham
6 slices Swiss cheese
¼ cup flour
¼ cup grated Parmesan cheese
½ tsp. rubbed sage
¼ tsp. paprika
¼ tsp. pepper
¼ cup vegetable oil
1 can cream of chicken soup
½ cup chicken broth
chopped fresh parsley for garnish, optional

Judge a man by his questions, not by his answers.

Flatten chicken to ⅛-inch thickness. Place ham and cheese on each breast. Roll up and tuck in ends; secure with a toothpick or several. Combine the flour, Parmesan cheese, sage, paprika, and pepper; coat chicken on all sides. Cover and refrigerate for 1 hour. In a large skillet, brown chicken in oil over medium-high heat. Transfer to 5-quart slow cooker. Combine soup and broth; pour over chicken. Cover and cook on low for 4–5 hours. Remove toothpicks. Garnish with parsley if desired. Yield: 6 servings.

Oven-Fried Buttermilk Chicken

1 cup flour
1½ tsp. poultry seasoning (optional)
1 tsp. paprika
½ tsp. seasoned salt
1 package of chicken pieces (2 breasts, 2 drumsticks, 2 thighs)
¾ cup buttermilk
¼ cup butter, melted

Dip chicken in buttermilk. Dredge chicken into mixed dry ingredients.

Drizzle melted butter onto rimmed baking sheet. Place chicken skin-down in pan and bake at 400° for 30 minutes. Carefully turn chicken and bake 30 minutes more.

Yost's Baked Chicken Pieces

From *Following Your Heart*

"I only have one request," Yost said, holding up his hand.
"Yes," Teresa said, her eyes on his bearded face.
"I would ask that you finish cleaning the house like you planned today," he said, "and that you perhaps make some food."
"We brought along a fresh loaf of bread," Teresa managed.
"Would that be okay for food?"
Yost smiled, "That would be a gut start, but I was hoping for a full supper with mashed potatoes, gravy, and maybe even a pie."

Every child has the right to be well fed and well led.

4 cups flour	2 tsp. onion powder
4 cups cracker crumbs	¼ cup vegetable oil
4 T. salt	20 lbs. chicken leg quarters
3 T. paprika	milk or buttermilk
2 T. sugar	2 sticks butter
2 tsp. garlic powder	

Mix first seven ingredients then mix in ¼ cup oil and refrigerate. When chilled, dip leg quarters in buttermilk then in flour mixture and place upside down in two cookie sheets with one stick of butter melted in each. Bake at 375° for 1 hour or 350° for 2 hours. Carefully flip chicken halfway through baking time.

Grandma's Barbecued Chicken

3 to 3½ lbs. chicken, cut into serving pieces	¼ cup lemon juice
	1 cup ketchup
shortening	2 T. Worcestershire sauce
1 small onion, chopped	1½ tsp. prepared mustard
1 T. vinegar	1 cup water
3 T. brown sugar	salt and pepper

Brown chicken in hot shortening. Remove. Brown onion in shortening and then add remaining ingredients. Simmer for about 30 minutes and then pour over the browned chicken in roaster. Bake at 350° for 1 hour or until done.

Note: Grandma would bake it till it was done then let it sit in a warm oven for up to 2 hours or so. Very good!

Parmesan Chicken

chicken pieces	½ cup water
3 eggs	½ cup chopped onion
3 T. water	1 tsp. garlic
3 cups flour	1 tsp. basil (optional)
1 T. Italian seasoning	1 tsp. oregano
shortening	mozzarella cheese
2 8-oz. cans tomato soup	Parmesan cheese

This recipe is for 2 skillets of chicken. Beat eggs and 3 tablespoons water. Roll chicken in eggs, then flour mixed with Italian seasoning. Brown in shortening. Mix soup, ½ cup water, onions, garlic, basil, and oregano. Pour over chicken. Cover and cook on low heat 45 minutes. Stir occasionally. Sprinkle mozzarella and Parmesan cheese over chicken before serving.

Apple Raisin Ham

1 T. flour
1 large oven roasting bag
4 medium tart apples, peeled
   and chopped
2 cups apple juice

1 cup raisins
½ cup brown sugar
1 tsp. cinnamon
1 boneless fully cooked ham
   (about 6 lbs.)

Shake flour in the oven roasting bag. Place in an ungreased 13 x 9-inch baking pan. Place the apples, apple juice, raisins, brown sugar, and cinnamon in the bag; mix well. Place ham in bag. Close bag and cut six ½-inch slits in the top.

Bake at 325° for 1¾ to 2 hours or until a thermometer registers 140°. Let ham stand for 10 minutes before slicing. Serve with sauce.

The kind word that falls today may not bear its fruit until tomorrow.

Duane's Parmesan Pork Roast

From *Missing Your Smile*

As she led him up the stairs, he said, "Wow, something sure smells good!"
"It's a roast. I hope you're hungry!"
"Of course," he said. "I can't wait."

1 boneless whole pork loin
   roast (4 lbs.)
⅔ cup grated Parmesan
   cheese
½ cup honey
3 T. soy sauce
2 T. dried basil

2 T. minced garlic
2 T. olive oil
½ tsp. salt
2 T. cornstarch
¼ cup water

Place roast in slow cooker cutting in half to fit if needed. Combine the cheese, honey, soy sauce, basil, garlic, oil, and salt; pour over pork. Cover and cook on low for 5½ to 6 hours or until done. Remove meat to a serving platter; keep warm. Skim fat from cooking juices; transfer to a small saucepan. Bring to a boil. Combine cornstarch and water until smooth. Gradually add to pan; stirring as you do so. Bring to a boil; cook and stir for 2 minutes or until thickened. Slice roast and serve with gravy.

Old-Fashioned Ham

The time to relax is when you don't have time for it.

1 whole, bone-in smoked ham (about 10 lbs.)	1½ T. apple cider vinegar
¼ tsp. salt	1 T. butter
1 T. flour	1 T. stone-ground mustard
½ cup water	1 stick cinnamon
juice and finely grated rind of 1 large orange	½ cup golden raisins
	2 T. maple syrup

Bake ham according to package directions. For sauce, combine salt and flour, gradually add water. Bring to a boil, stirring constantly until mixture becomes clear. Add remaining ingredients. Return to a boil and cook over medium heat about 20 minutes. Remove the cinnamon stick and discard. Pour sauce over ham during last 15 minutes of baking.

Barbecued Ribs

2 racks pork baby back ribs
(about 4½ lbs.)
1½ tsp. pepper
2½ cups barbecue sauce

¾ cup cherry preserves
1 T. Dijon mustard
1 garlic clove, minced

Cut the ribs into serving size pieces; sprinkle with pepper.
Place in a 5- or 6-quart slow cooker. Combine the remaining
ingredients; pour over the ribs. Cover and cook on low for 6–8
hours or until meat is tender. Serve with sauce.

Sunday Pot Roast

1 beef chuck pot roast (about
2½ lbs.)
salt and pepper
3 medium potatoes (about 1
lb.)
2 large carrots
1 large parsnip

2 large celery stalks
1 medium onion, sliced
2 bay leaves
1 tsp. dried rosemary
½ tsp. dried thyme
½ cup beef broth

Trim any excess fat from beef. Discard fat. Cut beef into serving-
size pieces; season with salt and pepper to taste. Scrub potatoes.
Cut into quarters. Cut carrots and parsnip diagonally into
¾-inch slices. Slice celery into 1½ to 2-inch pieces. Place potato,
carrot, parsnip, celery, onion, and bay leaves in slow cooker.
Sprinkle rosemary and thyme over vegetables. Arrange beef over
vegetables. Pour broth over beef. Cook on low about 8½ to 9
hours or until beef is fork-tender. Arrange all on serving platter
with juices.

If gravy is desired, bring juices to a boil. For each cup of juice,
mix ¼ cup of cold water and 2 tablespoons flour until smooth.
Add to boiling juices and cook and stir until thickened.

*When you
act like
a fool, a
true friend
doesn't think
you've done
a permanent
job.*

Aunt Betty's Country-Fried Venison

From *A Hope for Hannah*

Betty agreed… "You know how to marinate this meat. It makes a real tasty meat using the steaks."

"I don't have a recipe," Hannah said. "I'm sure you do, though."

Betty nodded. "Don't let me forget to give it to you before you go. You're staying for supper. A late supper."

2 lbs. venison tenderloin	1 egg, beaten
½ cup soy sauce	1 cup buttermilk
½ cup Worcestershire sauce	1 cup flour
½ cup butter, melted	2 tsp. seasoned salt
½ to 2 tsp. liquid smoke	2 tsp. vegetable oil

Cut tenderloin into about 1-inch thick slices. In a large resealable plastic bag, combine the soy sauce, Worcestershire sauce, butter, and liquid smoke. Add venison slices; seal bag and turn to coat. Refrigerate for 2 hours or more. In a shallow bowl, combine egg and buttermilk. In another bowl, combine flour and seasoned salt. Drain slices, discarding marinade. Dip slices in buttermilk mixture, then roll in flour mixture. In a large skillet, cook meat in oil for 12–14 minutes or until done, turning occasionally.

Venison Parmigiana

2 lbs. boneless venison steaks
1 egg
1 T. milk
⅔ cup seasoned bread crumbs
⅓ cup grated Parmesan
    cheese
5 T. vegetable oil
1 small onion, finely chopped

2 cups hot water
1 6-oz. can tomato paste
1 tsp. pepper
½ tsp. salt
½ tsp. sugar
½ tsp. dried marjoram
2 cups (8 oz.) shredded
    mozzarella cheese

Pound steaks to ¼-inch thickness; cut into serving-size pieces. In a shallow bowl, beat egg and milk. In another bowl, combine bread crumbs and Parmesan cheese. Dip venison in egg mixture, then coat with crumb mixture. In a large skillet, brown meat in oil on both sides. Place in a greased 13 x 9-inch baking dish. In the drippings, sauté onion for 2–3 minutes or until tender. Stir in the water, tomato paste, pepper, salt, sugar, and marjoram. Bring to a boil. Reduce heat; simmer uncovered, for 5 minutes. Pour over venison. Cover and bake at 350° for 50 minutes or until meat is tender. Uncover; sprinkle with cheese. Bake 10–15 minutes longer or until cheese is melted.

Idleness
causes
problems
only work
can solve.

Venison Tenderloins

¾ cup soy sauce
½ cup red wine vinegar
½ cup vegetable oil
⅓ cup lemon juice
¼ cup Worcestershire sauce

2 T. ground mustard
1½ tsp. dried parsley flakes
2 garlic cloves, minced
8 venison tenderloin steaks
    (about 4 oz. each)

In a resealable plastic bag, combine the first eight ingredients; add steaks. Seal bag and turn to coat; refrigerate for 8 hours or overnight. Drain and discard marinade. Grill steaks, uncovered, over medium-hot heat for 4 minutes on each side or until steaks are done to your choice.

Slow-Cooked Coffee Roast

1 boneless beef sirloin tip roast (about 2½ lbs.), cut in half
2 tsp. canola oil
1½ cups sliced fresh mushrooms
⅓ cup sliced green onions
2 garlic cloves, minced

1½ cups day-old brewed coffee
1 tsp. liquid smoke
½ tsp. salt
½ tsp. chili powder
¼ tsp. pepper
¼ cup cornstarch
⅓ cup cold water

A man shows what he is by doing what he does with what he has.

In a large nonstick skillet, brown roast on all sides in oil over medium-high heat. Place in a 5-quart slow cooker. In the same skillet, sauté mushrooms, onions, and garlic until tender; stir in coffee, liquid smoke, salt, chili powder, and pepper. Pour over roast. Cover and cook on low for 8–10 hours or until meat is tender. Remove roast and keep warm. Pour cooking juices into a 2-cup measuring cup; skim fat. Combine cornstarch and water until smooth. Gradually add 2 cups cooking juices. Bring to a boil; cook and stir for 2 minutes or until thickened. Serve with sliced beef.

Steak Fajitas

¼ cup orange juice
¼ cup white vinegar
4 garlic cloves, minced
1 tsp. seasoned salt
1 tsp. oregano
1 tsp. cumin
¼ tsp. cayenne pepper
1 lb. boneless beef sirloin
    steak, cut into ¼-inch
    strips

1 medium onion, thinly sliced
1 medium green pepper,
    thinly sliced
1 medium sweet red pepper,
    thinly sliced
2 T. vegetable oil, divided
4–6 flour tortillas (10 inches),
    warmed
shredded Cheddar cheese,
    picante sauce, and sour
    cream, optional

In a large resealable bag, combine the orange juice, vinegar, garlic, and seasonings; add the beef. Seal bag and turn to coat; set aside. In a large skillet, sauté onion and peppers in 1 tablespoon oil until crisp-tender; remove and set aside. Drain and discard marinade. In the same skillet, cook beef in remaining oil for 2–4 minutes or until it reaches desired doneness. Return vegetables to pan; heat through. Spoon meat and vegetables onto tortillas. If desired, top with cheese and serve with picante sauce and sour cream. Yield: 4–6 servings.

Beef and Snow Peas Salad

1 lb. flank steak
¼ cup ketchup
2 T. canola oil
2 T. lemon juice
1 T. brown sugar
¼ tsp. each garlic powder,
    garlic salt, ground ginger,
    and pepper
½ lb. fresh mushrooms, sliced

1 8-oz. can sliced water
    chestnuts, drained
1 onion, sliced into rings
1 cup fresh or frozen snow
    peas, thawed
2 medium tomatoes, cut into
    wedges
1 large head lettuce (about 12
    leaves)

Broil steak 4–6 inches from heat for 8–10 minutes on each side or until meat thermometer reads 170°. Cool completely. Thinly slice meat across the grain; place in resealable plastic bag. In a jar with a tight fitting lid, combine ketchup, oil, lemon juice, brown sugar, and seasonings; shake well. Pour over meat. Add mushrooms, water chestnuts, and onion. Turn to coat and refrigerate 8 hours or overnight. Add snow peas just before serving. Serve on lettuce leaves and garnish with tomatoes. Yield: 6 servings.

Slow-Cooked Short Ribs

A person who knows everything still has a lot to learn.

⅔ cup flour	¾ cup red wine vinegar
2 tsp. salt	¾ cup brown sugar
½ tsp. pepper	½ cup chili sauce
4 to 4½ lbs. boneless beef short ribs	⅓ cup ketchup
	⅓ cup Worcestershire sauce
¼ to ⅓ cup butter	5 garlic cloves, minced
1 large onion, chopped	1½ tsp. chili powder
1½ cups beef broth	

In a large resealable plastic bag, combine the flour, salt, and pepper. Add the ribs in batches and shake to coat. In a large skillet, brown ribs in butter. Transfer to a 6-quart slow cooker. In the same skillet, combine the remaining ingredients. Cook and stir until mixture comes to a boil; pour over ribs. Cover and cook on low for 8–10 hours or until meat is tender.

Liver with Peppers and Onions

½ cup flour
1 tsp. salt
¼ tsp. pepper
1 lb. liver, cut into bite-sized
    pieces
1 large onion, thinly sliced
    into rings
1 medium green pepper, cut
    into 1-inch pieces

1 sweet red pepper, cut into
    1-inch pieces
¼ cup vegetable oil, divided
1 T. cornstarch
1 cup beef broth
2 T. soy sauce
cooked rice or noodles

In a large resealable bag, combine the flour, salt, and pepper. Add liver; toss to coat. In a large skillet, cook onion and peppers in 2 tablespoons oil until crisp-tender. Remove from pan; set aside. In same skillet, cook and stir liver in remaining oil for 5–7 minutes or until no pink remains. In a small bowl, combine cornstarch, broth, and soy sauce until smooth; stir into liver. Bring to a boil; cook and stir for 2 minutes or until thickened. Return vegetables to the skillet; heat through. Serve over rice or noodles.

*Rather than
returning
a kindness,
pass it on.*

Sweet-and-Sour Meatballs

Meatballs:
1 lb. hamburger
½ cup dry bread crumbs
¼ cup milk
2 T. finely chopped onion
1 tsp. salt
½ tsp. Worcestershire sauce
1 egg

Sauce:
½ cup brown sugar
1 T. cornstarch
1 13¼-oz. can pineapple
    chunks, undrained
⅓ cup vinegar
1 T. soy sauce
1 small green pepper, coarsely
    chopped

Mix ingredients for meatballs; shape into twenty 1-inch balls. Cook in skillet; remove. For sauce, mix brown sugar and cornstarch. Stir in pineapple (with juice), vinegar, and soy sauce. Heat to boiling, stirring constantly; reduce heat. Add meatballs. Cover and simmer 10 minutes. Stir in green pepper. Cover; let simmer until crisp-tender, 5 minutes.

Salisbury Steak with Onion Gravy

2 eggs
1 10½-oz. can condensed French onion soup, divided
1 cup dry bread crumbs
½ tsp. salt
¼ tsp. pepper
3 lbs. ground beef or venison

1¼ cups water
½ cup ketchup
2 tsp. Worcestershire sauce
1 tsp. prepared mustard
1 package dry onion soup mix
1 can mushroom soup
⅔ cup half-and-half

Beat eggs. Stir in ⅔ cup of French onion soup, bread crumbs, salt, and pepper. Crumble beef or venison over mixture; mix gently. Shape into 12 oval patties. In a skillet, brown patties over medium heat for 3–4 minutes on each side. Remove and set aside; drain. Add the water, ketchup, Worcestershire sauce, mustard, onion soup mix, and remaining French onion soup to skillet. Bring to a boil. Return patties to skillet; spread with mushroom soup. Pour half-and-half over everything and cover. For venison, I let it sit on low most of the afternoon and then simmer it a bit before we eat. For beef, simmer for 15 minutes or until meat is no longer pink.

Sticky Bones

1 cup white vinegar
½ cup ketchup
½ cup honey
2 T. Worcestershire sauce
1 tsp. salt

1 tsp. ground mustard
1 tsp. paprika
1 garlic clove, minced
¼ tsp. pepper
4 lbs. bone-in beef short ribs

*We all need
something to
do, someone
to love, and
something
to hope for.*

In a saucepan, combine all ingredients except meat. Bring to a boil. Reduce heat; cover and simmer for 15 minutes. Set aside 1 cup for basting. Cool remaining marinade. Pour the remaining marinade in a large resealable plastic bag; add ribs. Seal bag and turn to coat; refrigerate for at least 2 hours. Drain and discard marinade. Bake ribs, uncovered, at 325° for 1 hour or until meat is tender, basting frequently with reserved marinade.

Little Cheddar Meatloaves

1 egg
½ to ¾ cup milk
4 oz. shredded Cheddar
    cheese
½ cup quick cooking oats
½ cup chopped onion

1 tsp. salt
1 lb. ground beef
⅔ cup ketchup
½ cup brown sugar
1½ tsp. mustard

Beat egg and milk. Stir in cheese, oats, onion, and salt. Add beef and mix well. Shape into 8 loaves. Place in a greased 13 x 9-inch pan. Combine ketchup, brown sugar, and mustard. Spoon over loaves. Bake uncovered at 350° for 45 minutes or until done.

Parmesan-Baked Salmon

½ cup mayonnaise
¼ cup Parmesan cheese
¼ tsp. red pepper

8 salmon fillets (2 lbs.), skin removed
4 tsp. lemon juice
20 Ritz crackers, crushed

Preheat oven to 400°. Mix mayonnaise, cheese, and pepper. Place salmon on foil-lined cookie sheet. Drizzle evenly with lemon juice. Top with cheese mixture. Sprinkle with crackers. Bake 12–15 minutes.

Special Thanksgiving Turkey

1 turkey

Brine:
1 gallon water
¾–1 cup Tenderquick

Gravy:
1 quart broth
½ cup flour
1 egg yolk

For a no-hassle Thanksgiving, prepare brine Saturday evening. Sunday morning put in frozen turkey. (For a 12–15 lb. turkey make 1½ batches of brine. For a larger turkey make 2 batches.) Soak in refrigerator 3 days and 3 nights. On Wednesday, roast turkey in cooking bag at 250° until done (approximately 5½–6 hours for 12–15 lb. turkey; 9 hours for a larger turkey). When done let set for 20 minutes then drain off broth and reserve. Let turkey cool several hours then debone, cutting in slices. Use all of broth from turkey to make gravy. Put turkey slices and gravy in alternate layers in roaster. Refrigerate. On Thursday— Thanksgiving Day—bake until hot, approximately 1 hour at 350°. No salt needed.

Chicken Parmigiana

4 boneless, skinless chicken
    breast halves
1 6-oz. can tomato paste
¾ cup water
2 garlic cloves, minced
1 T. dried parsley flakes
1 tsp. salt

¼ tsp. Italian seasoning
½ tsp. dried oregano
¼ tsp. crushed red pepper
2 cups (8 oz.) shredded
    mozzarella cheese
¼ cup grated Parmesan
    cheese

Place chicken in a greased 8-inch square pan. In a saucepan, combine tomato paste, water, garlic, and seasonings; bring to a boil. Pour over chicken. Bake uncovered for 15–20 minutes at 400°. Sprinkle with cheese. Bake 10 minutes longer or until cheese is melted.

Pork Chops with Scalloped Potatoes

3 T. butter
3 T. flour
1½ tsp. salt
¼ tsp. pepper
1 14½-oz. can chicken broth
6 rib or loin pork chops
    (¾-inch thick)

2 T. cooking oil
additional salt and pepper,
    optional
6 cups thinly sliced peeled
    potatoes (about 4 lbs.)
1 medium onion, sliced

In a saucepan, melt butter; stir in flour, salt, and pepper. Add chicken broth; cook and stir constantly until mixture boils. Cook 1 minute; remove from heat and set aside.

Brown pork chops in oil; season to taste with additional salt and pepper if desired. In a greased 13 x 9-inch pan, layer potatoes and onion. Pour broth mixture over them. Place pork chops on top. Cover and bake at 350° for 1 hour; uncover and bake 30 minutes longer or until potatoes are tender.

The deacon was sent out by the bishop on
Saturday afternoon to speak with Leo and Leona
Troyer about their Ordnung transgression.
"Did you not fly the plane out to Oregon
the other week?" the deacon asked.
"No," Leo said, as Leona shook her head. "There
was someone else called a pilot flying the thing."
"I see," the deacon said. "I guess that
does make it a less serious matter."

PIES

Hannah's Pecan Pie

From *A Baby for Hannah*

*Jake ate his supper slowly as Hannah watched his face.
"I made pecan pie today," Hannah said. "Especially for you."
He smiled weakly, briefly meeting her eyes.*

3 eggs

⅓ cup butter, melted

1 cup light corn syrup

½ tsp. salt

⅔ cup sugar

1 cup pecan halves

1 unbaked pie crust

Beat first five ingredients on low speed slightly or with hand beater. Stir in pecan halves. Pour into pie crust. Bake at 375° for 40–50 minutes.

Pie Crust

⅓ cup plus 1 T. shortening

1 cup flour

½ tsp. salt

2 to 3 T. ice water

Mix flour and salt. Cut shortening into flour and salt until particles are pea-sized. Sprinkle in water a bit at a time, mixing with fork until all flour is moistened and pastry cleans side of bowl.

Note: I do not always use quite as much shortening as it says and I really like the effect of ice water better as opposed to just cold water. Do not over mix.

For double-crust pies, I moisten the top crust with milk and sprinkle with sugar. For a more buttery flavor use butter-flavored shortening.

Every time you turn green with envy, you are ripe for trouble.

Never-Fail Pie Crust

1 cup flour
¼ tsp. salt
⅓ cup shortening

1½ tsp. white vinegar
2 to 3 T. milk

Mix flour and salt; cut in shortening until mixture resembles coarse crumbs. Sprinkle with vinegar. Gradually add milk, tossing with a fork until ball forms. Cover and refrigerate for 30 minutes or until easy to handle. Makes a single crust.

The brightest lightning comes from the darkest clouds, and the purest faith from life's severest trials.

Raspberry Custard Pie

Pastry for single-crust pie
3 eggs
2 cups sugar
½ cup flour
⅓ cup evaporated milk
2 tsp. vanilla
dash salt
5½ cups fresh or frozen
    raspberries

Topping:
½ cup flour
¼ cup brown sugar
¼ cup cold butter

Line a 9-inch pie plate with pastry. Beat eggs. Add the sugar, flour, milk, vanilla, and salt; mix well. Gently fold in raspberries. Pour into crust.

For topping: Combine flour and brown sugar; cut in butter until crumbly. Sprinkle over filling. Bake at 400° for 10 minutes. Reduce heat to 350°; bake 45 to 50 minutes longer or until knife inserted near center comes out clean.

Apple Cream Pie

pastry for 1 pie
tart apples, sliced or shoe
    stringed (about 2 cups)
1 cup sugar

3 T. flour
1 cup half-and-half
cinnamon

Put apples in unbaked pie crust. Mix sugar and flour; add half-and-half. Pour over apples and sprinkle with cinnamon. Bake at 350° for 15 minutes; then turn down to 325° or lower to finish (15–25 minutes longer) or until set.

Rhubarb Custard Pie

2 eggs, separated
1¼ cups sugar, divided
2 T. flour
1 cup cream

1 tsp. vanilla
1½ cups rhubarb
1 unbaked pie shell
2 T. butter

Beat egg yolks. In a separate bowl, mix sugar and flour; add egg yolks and cream well. Add cream and vanilla. Put rhubarb into pie shell and pour cream mixture over rhubarb. Dot with butter. Bake at 375° for 30-45 minutes. Cover with meringue made from 2 egg whites and ¼ cup sugar beaten until stiff peaks form. Put back in oven until meringue is nice and brown (approximately 15 minutes).

Ruth's Caramel Custard Pie

1 unbaked pie shell
1 T. flour (heaping)
¾ cup sugar
2 eggs, separated
pinch of salt

1 cup cream
1 cup milk
½ tsp. maple flavoring
chopped nuts (pecans or
    English walnuts)

Mix flour, sugar, egg yolks, and salt. Add enough cream to make a paste. Bring milk and rest of cream to scalding and add to other ingredients. (Do not cool milk.) Beat egg whites until stiff and fold in last along with maple flavoring. Pour into pie shell; sprinkle with nuts. Bake at 375° for 10 minutes then at 325° until done (approximately 45–50 minutes). (You do not want it to boil while in the oven so turn it lower if needed.)

No man is so wise that he knows everything, nor is any man so stupid he knows nothing.

Hannah's Cherry Pie

From *A Hope for Hannah*

As he downed his last piece of cherry pie, Roy thumped his stomach and pronounced himself satisfied.

pastry for 2-crust pie
1 can cherry pie filling (I like
    the one with more fruit)
¼ tsp. almond extract

1–1½ tsp. butter
milk
sugar

Mix almond extract with pie filling; pour into crust. Dot with butter. When top crust is on, brush with milk and sprinkle with sugar. Put on bottom rack in the oven and bake at 400° for 30–45 minutes.

Old-Time Custard Pie

For 8-inch pie:	*For 9-inch pie:*
3 eggs	4 eggs
⅓ cup sugar	⅔ cup sugar
¼ tsp. salt	½ tsp. salt
¼ tsp. nutmeg	¼ tsp. nutmeg
1¾ cups milk	2⅔ cups milk
1 tsp. vanilla	1 tsp. vanilla

Heat oven to 425°. Beat eggs slightly; beat in remaining ingredients. Pour into pastry-lined plate. Bake 20 minutes. Reduce temperature to 325°. Bake until knife inserted halfway between crust and center and edge comes out clean, 10–20 minutes longer.

An ounce of work is worth a ton of wishing.

Fresh Apple Pie

For 8-inch pie:	*For 9-inch pie:*
½ cup sugar	¾ cup sugar
3 T. flour	¼ cup flour
¼ tsp. nutmeg	½ tsp. nutmeg
¼ tsp. cinnamon	½ tsp. cinnamon
dash of salt	dash of salt
5 cups thinly sliced pared tart apples	6 cups thinly sliced pared tart apples
1 T. butter	2 T. butter

Heat oven to 400°. Mix sugar, flour, nutmeg, cinnamon, and salt. Stir in apples. Turn into pie shell; dot with butter. Cover with top crust that has slits in it. Brush with milk and sprinkle with sugar. Bake 40–50 minutes.

Ruth's Toffee Bits Pie

1 8-oz. package cream cheese, softened
2 T. sugar
½ cup half-and-half cream
1 8-oz. carton whipped topping

1 8-oz. package milk chocolate English toffee bits, divided
1 graham cracker crust (9 inches)

Beat cream cheese and sugar until smooth. Beat in cream until blended. Fold in whipped topping and 1 cup toffee bits. Spoon into crust; sprinkle with remaining toffee bits. Cover and freeze overnight. Remove from freezer 15 minutes before serving.

Potluck Apple Pie

2¼ cups flour, divided
¼ cup water
pinch salt
1 cup shortening

Filling:
½ cup maple syrup, divided
3 lbs. tart apples (8-9 medium), peeled and thinly sliced

1¼ cups sugar
¼ cup lemon juice
2 tsp. cinnamon
1 tsp. vanilla

Topping:
1 cup flour
½ cup brown sugar
½ cup butter
1 cup chopped pecans

Combine ¼ cup flour and water until smooth; set aside. Combine salt and remaining flour; cut in shortening until mixture resembles coarse crumbs. Add reserved flour mixture; knead gently until dough forms a ball. Press dough onto the bottom and up the sides of an ungreased 15 x 10 x 1-inch baking pan. Spread ¼ cup syrup over crust. Arrange apples over syrup.

Combine sugar, lemon juice, cinnamon, vanilla, and remaining syrup; drizzle over apples.

For topping: Combine flour and sugar. Cut in butter until mixture resembles coarse crumbs. Stir in pecans. Sprinkle over filling. Bake at 350° for 1 hour or until apples are tender.

Ice Cream-Strawberry Pie

Crust:
3 T. butter, melted
1 10-oz. package regular marshmallows or 4 cups miniature marshmallows
6 cups crisp rice cereal

Filling:
vanilla ice cream

Topping:
chopped and crushed fresh strawberries, sweetened with sugar

To be able to look at one's past with satisfaction is to live twice.

Add marshmallows to butter and cook on low heat until melted, stirring most of the time. Remove from heat and stir in rice cereal. Press into two buttered pie plates. Fill with vanilla ice cream and freeze if not ready to use. When ready to serve top with strawberries. Yummy and simple. I remember my mom serving this after we finished putting up hay.

Peanut Butter Pie

6 cups milk, divided
1½ cups sugar
½ cup cornstarch
1 tsp. salt
6 egg yolks

2 tsp. vanilla
3 cups powdered sugar
¾ cup peanut butter
2 baked pie shells
whipped topping or
    sweetened whipped cream

For filling, heat 5 cups milk and sugar to boiling point. Meanwhile, mix cornstarch and salt; add remaining 1 cup milk. Mix in egg yolks, then add vanilla. Pour into boiling milk and sugar and continue beating occasionally. Boil until thick and smooth. Remove from heat and cool.

Mix together powdered sugar and peanut butter until crumbly. Put ⅔ cup of crumbs in each pie shell. Fill with pudding and add another layer of crumbs, saving some to sprinkle on top. Top with whipped topping and sprinkle with remaining crumbs. Note: You may use instant vanilla pudding made according to package directions for the pudding.

Shoo-Fly Pie

2 cups flour
1½ cups brown sugar
2 T. butter
2 T. shortening
1¼ cups King syrup
½ cup pancake syrup

¼ cup molasses
2 eggs, beaten
2 tsp. baking soda
1½ cups boiling water
2 unbaked pie shells

For crumbs, mix flour and brown sugar; cut in butter and shortening. Reserve 2 cups of these crumbs. To the remaining crumbs add syrups, molasses, and eggs. Dissolve soda in water and add to syrup mixture. Pour into pie crusts and sprinkle with 1 cup crumbs on each pie. Bake at 350° for 45–60 minutes.

Miriam's Pumpkin Pie

⅔ cup sugar
⅓ cup brown sugar
1½ T. flour
1 tsp. cinnamon
¼ tsp. nutmeg
½ tsp. ginger

½ tsp. salt
1 cup pumpkin
3 eggs, separated
1½ cups evaporated milk
2 unbaked pie shells
whipped topping or cream,
    whipped and sweetened

Mix sugars, flour, and seasonings. Add pumpkin, egg yolks, and evaporated milk. Beat egg whites until stiff; fold into pumpkin mixture. Pour into pie shells. Bake at 425° for 10 minutes, then reduce heat to 325° and bake 45 minutes longer. Cool. Top with whipped topping if desired.

Southern Sweet Potato Pie

3 T. flour
1⅔ cups sugar
1 cup mashed sweet potatoes
2 eggs
¼ cup light corn syrup

¼ tsp. nutmeg
pinch salt
½ cup butter, softened
¾ cup evaporated milk
1 unbaked pie shell (9 inches)

Combine flour and sugar. Add the sweet potatoes, eggs, corn syrup, nutmeg, salt, butter, and evaporated milk; beat well. Pour into pastry shell. Bake at 350° for 55–60 minutes. Cool on wire rack for 1 hour. Refrigerate for at least 3 hours before serving.

*If a dollar
doesn't
do what
it used to,
remember
that hardly
anyone else
does either.*

Lemon Meringue Pie

1¼ cups sugar
6 T. cornstarch
2 cups water
3 egg yolks, beaten
3 T. butter, cubed
⅓ cup lemon juice
2 tsp. white vinegar
1½ tsp. lemon extract
1 pie shell (9 inches), baked

Meringue:
½ cup plus 2 T. water
1 T. cornstarch
3 egg whites
1 tsp. vanilla extract
pinch salt
6 T. sugar

Take life as you find it, but don't leave it so.

In a large saucepan, combine sugar and cornstarch. Stir in water until smooth. Cook and stir over medium-high heat until thickened and bubbly. Reduce heat to low; cook and stir 2 minutes longer. Remove from the heat. Stir 1 cup of hot filling into egg yolks; return all to the pan, stirring constantly. Bring to a gentle boil; cook and stir for 2 minutes. Remove from the heat. Stir in the butter. Gently stir in lemon juice, vinegar, and lemon extract. Pour hot filling into pastry shell.

For meringue, combine water and cornstarch in a saucepan until smooth. Cook and stir until thickened and clear, about 2 minutes. Meanwhile, beat the egg whites, vanilla, and salt on medium speed until soft peaks form. Gradually beat in sugar, 1 tablespoon at a time, on high until stiff glossy peaks form and sugar is dissolved. Gradually add cornstarch mixture, beating well on high. Immediately spread over hot filling, sealing edges to crust. Bake at 350° for 12–15 minutes or until meringue is golden brown. Cool on wire rack for 1 hour. Refrigerate for at least 3 hours before serving.

Festive Fruit Tart

pastry for single-crust pie
(9 inches)
1 package (8 oz.) cream
cheese, softened
3 T. sugar
1 tsp. vanilla extract
¾ tsp. almond extract,
divided

1 cup fresh blueberries
1 cup fresh raspberries
1 medium ripe peach or
nectarine, peeled and
sliced
2 T. apricot preserves

Press pastry onto the bottom and up the sides of an ungreased 9-inch tart pan with a removable bottom; trim edges. Generously prick the bottom with a fork. Bake at 425° for 10–12 minutes or until golden brown. Cool completely. Beat cream cheese, sugar, vanilla, and ½ teaspoon almond extract until smooth; spread over crust. Arrange fruit over cream cheese mixture. Combine apricot preserves and the remaining ¼ teaspoon almond extract. Microwave uncovered on high for 20–30 seconds or until warm; brush over fruit. Refrigerate until ready to serve.

White Chocolate Fruit Tart

¾ cup butter, softened
½ cup powdered sugar
1½ cups flour
1 package (10–12 oz.) vanilla
or white chips, melted and
cooled
¼ cup heavy whipping cream
1 package (8 oz.) cream
cheese, softened
1 can (20 oz.) pineapple
chunks, undrained

1 pint fresh strawberries,
sliced
1 can (11 oz.) mandarin
oranges, drained
2 kiwis, peeled and sliced
3 T. sugar
2 tsp. cornstarch
½ tsp. lemon juice

Cream butter and powdered sugar until light and fluffy. Gradually add flour; mix well. Press into an ungreased 11-inch tart pan with removable bottom or 12-inch pizza pan with sides. Bake at 300° for 25–30 minutes or until lightly browned. Cool.

For filling, beat melted chips and cream. Add cream cheese and beat until smooth. Spread over crust and refrigerate for 30 minutes. Drain pineapple, reserving ½ cup juice; set juice aside. Arrange the pineapple, berries, oranges, and kiwi over filling.

For glaze, combine sugar and cornstarch in a saucepan. Stir in lemon juice and reserved pineapple juice until smooth. Bring to a boil over medium heat; cook and stir for 2 minutes or until thickened. Cool; brush over fruit. Refrigerate for 1 hour before serving.

God will never let anything come your way that you and He can't handle.

Green Tomato Pie

1½ cups sugar
5 T. flour
1 tsp. cinnamon
pinch salt
3 cups thinly sliced green tomatoes (about 4–5 medium)

1 T. cider vinegar
pastry for double-crust pie
1 T. butter
2 tsp. milk
sugar

In a bowl, combine the sugar, flour, cinnamon, and salt. Add tomatoes and vinegar; toss to coat. Line a pie plate with bottom crust. Add filling; dot with butter. Roll out remaining crust; cutting out design of your choice. Put on top of pie, sealing and fluting edges. Brush milk over top; sprinkle liberally with sugar. Bake at 350° for 1 hour or until tomatoes are tender. Cool.

QUICK BREADS

Banana Nut Bread

2½ cups flour
½ cup sugar
½ cup brown sugar
3½ tsp. baking powder
1 tsp. salt

3 T. oil
⅓ cup milk
1¼ cups mashed bananas
1 egg
1 cup chopped walnuts

Mix all ingredients. Beat 30 seconds. Pour into loaf pans with only bottoms greased. Bake at 350° for 1 hour or so until toothpick inserted in center comes out clean. Cool slightly then remove from pan and cool completely on wire rack. Will keep in refrigerator for a week. Can also be frozen.

Moist Banana Bread

2½ cups flour
1¼ cups sugar
2 packages (3.4 oz. each) instant vanilla pudding mix
1¼ tsp. baking soda
1 tsp. salt

1 tsp. cinnamon
5 eggs
2 cups mashed ripe bananas
1 cup canola oil
1 tsp. vanilla
1 cup chopped nuts, optional

In a large bowl, combine the first six ingredients. In a bowl, whisk the eggs, bananas, oil, and vanilla. Stir into dry ingredients just until moistened. Stir in nuts if desired. Transfer to two greased 8 x 4-inch loaf pans. Bake at 350° for 55–65 minutes or until toothpick inserted near the center comes out clean. Cool for 10 minutes before removing from pans.

Cappuccino Muffins

Espresso Spread:
4 oz. cream cheese, cubed and
   softened
1 T. sugar
½ tsp. instant coffee granules
½ tsp. vanilla
¼ cup miniature semisweet
   chocolate chips

Muffins:
2 cups flour
¾ cup sugar
2½ tsp. baking powder
1 tsp. cinnamon
½ tsp. salt
1 cup milk
2 T. instant coffee granules
½ cup butter, melted
1 egg
1 tsp. vanilla
¾ cup miniature semisweet
   chocolate chips

*We are
seldom
aware of
what's
cooking
until the pot
boils over.*

In a food processor or blender, combine the spread ingredients; cover and process until well blended. Transfer to a small bowl; cover and refrigerate until serving. For muffins, combine the flour, sugar, baking powder, cinnamon, and salt. In a small bowl, stir milk and coffee granules until granules are dissolved. Add butter, egg, and vanilla; mix well. Stir into dry ingredients just until moistened. Fold in chocolate chips.

Fill greased or paper-lined muffin cups two-thirds full. Bake at 375° for 17–20 minutes or until toothpick comes out clean. Cool for 5 minutes before removing from pans. Serve with espresso spread.

Pumpkin Cream Cheese Muffins

Filling:
1 8-oz. package cream cheese, softened
1 cup powdered sugar

Muffins:
3 cups flour
1 tsp. cinnamon
1 tsp. nutmeg
1 tsp. cloves
1 T. plus 1 tsp. pumpkin pie spice

1 tsp. salt
1 tsp. baking soda
4 large eggs
2 cups sugar
2 cups pumpkin puree
1¼ cups vegetable oil

Topping:
½ cup sugar
5 T. flour
1½ tsp. cinnamon
4 T. cold butter

For filling, combine the cream cheese and powdered sugar; mix well. Transfer to a piece of plastic wrap and shape into a log about 1½ inches in diameter. Smooth plastic wrap tightly around the log, and reinforce with a piece of foil. Transfer to freezer and chill until at least slightly firm, at least 2 hours.

For muffins, preheat oven to 350°. Line muffin pans with paper liners. Combine the flour, cinnamon, nutmeg, cloves, pumpkin pie spice, salt, and baking soda. In another bowl, combine eggs, sugar, pumpkin puree, and oil. Mix on medium-low speed until blended. With mixer on low speed, add dry ingredients just until incorporated. For topping, combine sugar, flour, and cinnamon. Cut in butter until mixture is coarse and crumbly. Transfer to refrigerator until ready to use.

To assemble muffins, fill each muffin cup with a small amount of batter, just enough to cover the bottom of the liner (1–2 tablespoons). Slice the log of cream cheese filling into 24 equal pieces. Place a slice of the cream cheese mixture into each muffin cup. Divide remaining batter among the muffin cups, placing on top of cream cheese to cover completely. Sprinkle a small amount of the topping mixture over each of the muffin cups. Bake 20–25 minutes.

The greatest of faults is to be conscious of none.

All-Star Muffin Mix

Mix:
8 cups flour
3 cups sugar
3 T. baking powder
2 tsp. salt
2 tsp. cinnamon

2 tsp. nutmeg

For plain muffins:
1 egg
1 cup 2% milk
½ cup butter, melted

Place 2¾ cups muffin mix in bowl. Whisk the egg, milk, and butter; stir into dry ingredients just until moistened. Fill paper-lined muffin cups ¾ full. Bake at 400° for 18–21 minutes or until toothpick comes out clean. Cool for 5 minutes before removing from pan.

For banana muffins:

Whisk 1 cup mashed ripe bananas with liquids as for plain muffins and continue as with plain muffins.

For blueberry muffins:

After muffins are mixed as for plain muffins, fold in 1 cup fresh or frozen blueberries.

For cranberry-pecan muffins:

Add 1 cup chopped fresh or frozen cranberries, ½ cup chopped pecans, and 3 tablespoons sugar to the dry mix. Then continue as for plain muffins.

For apricot-cherry muffins:

Add ½ cup chopped dried apricots and ½ cup dried cherries to the dry mix. Then continue as for plain muffins.

For cappuccino muffins:

Add 1 cup miniature semisweet chocolate chips and 2 teaspoons instant coffee granules to the dry mix. Then continue as for plain muffins.

For carrot-raisin muffins:

Add ¾ cup shredded carrots and ⅓ cup golden raisins to dry mix. Then continue as for plain muffins.

For apple-cheese muffins:

Add ½ cup shredded peeled apple and ½ cup shredded Colby-Jack cheese to dry mix. Continue as for plain muffins.

For rhubarb-orange muffins:

Add ¾ cup diced fresh or frozen rhubarb and ⅓ cup orange marmalade to dry mix. Continue as for plain muffins.

Golden Corn Bread

1 cup cornmeal	4 tsp. baking powder
1 cup flour	1 egg
¼ cup sugar	1 cup milk
½ tsp. salt	¼ cup soft shortening

Mix dry ingredients; add the rest of the ingredients. Beat about 1 minute. Pour into greased 8-inch square pan and bake at 400° for 20–25 minutes or until toothpick comes out clean. I often add a bit more sugar.

Maple-Nut Twists

2 cups flour
1 T. sugar
1 T. baking powder
½ tsp. cream of tartar
¼ tsp. salt
½ cup firm butter
¾ cup milk

Filling:
¼ cup chopped nuts
2 T. butter, softened
2 T. maple-flavored syrup
½ tsp. ground cinnamon

Maple glaze:
1 cup powdered sugar
1 to 2 T. milk
½ tsp. maple flavor

Heat oven to 450°. Grease cookie sheet. Mix flour, sugar, baking powder, cream of tartar, and salt. Cut in ½ cup butter until mixture looks like coarse crumbs. Add ¾ cup milk and stir with fork just until moistened.

On lightly floured surface, knead dough 10–12 times or until almost smooth. Pat or roll dough into 15 x 9-inch rectangle. Mix filling ingredients. Spread filling over dough. Fold dough lengthwise in half to make 15 x 4½-inch rectangle. Cut rectangle crosswise into fifteen 1-inch strips. Twist each strip twice. Place on cookie sheet, pressing both ends down. Bake 10–12 minutes or until golden brown. Cool on cookie sheets 1–2 minutes. Remove to wire rack. Mix glaze ingredients, adding milk if necessary until thin enough to drizzle. Drizzle glaze over warm twists.

Cinnamon Biscuits

2 cups flour
1 T. baking powder
1 tsp. salt
¼ tsp. baking soda
¼ cup vegetable oil

¾ cup buttermilk
½ cup butter, softened
¾ cup sugar
1 tsp. cinnamon
1 cup milk, optional

Combine flour, baking powder, salt, and baking soda. Stir in vegetable oil. Add buttermilk and stir just until blended. Knead dough on a lightly floured surface until smooth. Roll dough into a 15 x 8-inch rectangle. Preheat the oven to 400°. Grease a 9-inch round baking pan lightly.

Spread butter over the dough. Combine sugar and cinnamon. Sprinkle over butter. Roll up rectangle, jelly roll style, starting from one long side. Pinch seam to seal. Cut the roll into 1½-inch slices. Arrange the slices, cut side up, in prepared baking pan. Bake until lightly browned, about 15 to 20 minutes. Remove from oven. Pour milk over the top, if desired. Serve hot.

Light as a Feather Muffins

⅓ cup shortening
½ cup sugar
1 egg
1½ cups cake flour or
    all-purpose flour
1½ tsp. baking powder
½ tsp. salt

¼ tsp. nutmeg
½ cup milk

Topping:
½ cup sugar
1 tsp. cinnamon
½ cup butter, melted

Cream together the shortening, sugar, and egg. Combine dry ingredients; add to creamed egg mixture alternately with milk. Fill greased muffin tins ⅔ full. Bake at 325° for 20–25 minutes or until golden. Let cool for 3–4 minutes. Meanwhile, combine sugar and cinnamon in a small bowl. Roll warm muffins in melted butter, then in sugar mixture. Serve warm. Yield: 8–10 muffins. My family likes these cold too.

Colonial Gingerbread

2 cups flour	1 cup molasses
¾ cup buttermilk	½ cup sugar
½ cup butter, softened	1 egg
1 tsp. baking soda	1 tsp. ginger
1 tsp. cinnamon	

Grease and flour 9 x 9-inch pan. Beat all ingredients until blended. Bake 1 hour. Delicious with strawberries and whipped cream.

It's better to sleep over what you plan to do than to be kept awake at night by what you have done.

Garlic Cheese Biscuits

2 cups flour	½ cup butter-flavored
3 tsp. garlic powder, divided	shortening
2½ tsp. baking powder	¾ cup shredded Cheddar
½ tsp. baking soda	cheese
½ tsp. chicken bouillon	1 cup buttermilk
granules	3 T. butter, melted

Combine the flour, 2 teaspoons garlic powder, baking powder, baking soda, and bouillon; cut in shortening until mixture is crumbly. Add cheese. Stir in buttermilk just until moistened.

Drop by heaping teaspoonfuls onto a greased baking sheet. Bake at 425° for 10 minutes. Combine the butter and remaining garlic powder; brush over biscuits. Bake 4 minutes longer or until golden brown. Serve warm.

Cornmeal Cheddar Biscuits

1½ cups flour
½ cup cornmeal
3 tsp. baking powder
2 tsp. sugar

¼ to ½ tsp. salt
½ cup cold butter
½ cup shredded Cheddar
   cheese
1 cup milk

Combine the flour, cornmeal, baking powder, sugar, and salt. Cut in butter until mixture is crumbly. Stir in cheese and milk just until moistened. Drop by ¼ cupfuls 2 inches apart onto an ungreased baking sheet. Bake at 425° for 12–15 minutes or until golden brown. Serve warm.

*Throw mud
and you
will have
dirty hands,
whether the
mud hits the
mark or not.*

Zucchini Oat Muffins

2½ cups flour
1½ cups sugar
1 cup chopped pecans
½ cup quick-cooking oats
3 tsp. baking powder

1 tsp. salt
1 tsp. cinnamon
4 eggs
1 medium zucchini, shredded
   (about ¾ cup)
¾ cup vegetable oil

Combine the flour, sugar, pecans, oats, baking powder, salt, and cinnamon. Beat the eggs; add zucchini and oil. Stir into dry ingredients just until moistened (batter will be lumpy). Fill greased muffin cups three-fourths full. Bake at 400° for 20–25 minutes or until toothpick comes out clean. Cool for 5 minutes before removing from pan.

Banana Chip Muffins

1 egg
⅓ cup vegetable oil
¾ cup sugar
3 medium ripe bananas,
    mashed (about 1⅓ cups)
2 cups flour

½ cup old-fashioned oats
¾ tsp. baking soda
½ tsp. baking powder
½ tsp. salt
¾ cup miniature semisweet
    chocolate chips

Beat egg, oil, and sugar until smooth. Stir in bananas. Combine the flour, oats, baking soda, baking powder, and salt; stir into the banana mixture just until moistened. Stir in chocolate chips. Fill greased muffin cups three-fourths full. Bake at 375° for 18–20 minutes or until toothpick comes out clean. Cool for 5 minutes before removing from pan.

*Sorrow is
the pick
which mines
the heart for
joy to fill.*

Apple Streusel Muffins

1½ cups flour
¼ cup sugar
2 tsp. baking powder
½ tsp. cinnamon
¼ tsp. salt
⅛ tsp. nutmeg
1 egg
½ cup milk
¼ cup vegetable oil

1 cup peeled and shredded
    tart apple

Streusel topping:
⅓ cup brown sugar
2 T. flour
½ tsp. cinnamon
2 T. butter, softened
⅓ cup chopped pecans

Combine the flour, sugar, baking powder, cinnamon, salt, and nutmeg. In a small bowl, whisk the egg, milk, and oil. Stir into dry ingredients just until moistened. Fold in apples. In another bowl, combine the topping ingredients. Set aside 3 tablespoons of the topping. Spoon half of the batter into 12 greased muffin cups. Sprinkle with the remaining topping. Cover with enough batter to fill muffin cups two-thirds full. Sprinkle with reserved topping. Bake at 400° for 20–25 minutes or until toothpick comes out clean. Cool for 5 minutes before removing from pan.

Zucchini Chip Bread

3 cups flour
2 cups sugar
1 tsp. baking soda
1 tsp. salt
1 tsp. nutmeg
½ tsp. cinnamon
¼ tsp. baking powder
3 eggs

½ cup unsweetened applesauce
½ cup vegetable oil
1 T. grated orange peel
2 tsp. vanilla
2 cups shredded zucchini
1 cup chopped walnuts
1 cup (6 oz.) semisweet chocolate chips

Combine first 7 ingredients. In another bowl, beat eggs, applesauce, oil, orange peel, and vanilla. Stir into dry ingredients just until moistened. Fold in zucchini, nuts, and chocolate chips. Transfer to two greased loaf pans. Bake at 350° for 55–60 minutes or until toothpick comes out clean. Cool for 10 minutes before removing from pan. Cool completely.

Blessed is the person who is too busy to worry in the daytime and too tired to worry at night.

Pumpkin Spice Bread

3 cups sugar
1 cup vegetable oil
4 eggs, lightly beaten
1 15-oz. can pumpkin
3½ cups flour
1 tsp. baking soda
1 tsp. salt

1 tsp. cinnamon
1 tsp. nutmeg
½ tsp. baking powder
½ tsp. cloves
½ tsp. allspice
½ cup water

Combine the sugar, oil, and eggs. Add pumpkin and mix well.
Combine the dry ingredients; add to the pumpkin mixture
alternately with the water, beating well after each addition. Pour
into two greased loaf pans. Bake at 350° for 60–65 minutes or
until a toothpick comes out clean. Cool for 10 minutes before
removing from pans.

Cranberry-Pecan Muffins

1½ cups fresh or frozen
    cranberries
1¼ cups sugar, divided
3 cups flour
4½ tsp. baking powder
½ tsp. salt

½ cup butter
2 eggs, lightly beaten
1 cup milk
1 cup pecans, chopped
1 T. grated lemon peel,
    optional

Toss cranberries with ¼ cup sugar; set aside. Combine flour,
baking powder, salt, and remaining sugar. Cut in butter until
mixture resembles coarse crumbs. Combine eggs and milk; stir
into flour mixture just until moistened. Fold in pecans, lemon
peel, and cranberries. Fill greased or paper-lined muffin cups
two-thirds full. Bake at 400° for 20–25 minutes or until done.
Makes about 18 muffins.

Cranberry Corn Bread

½ cup butter, softened
1 cup sugar
2 eggs
1½ cups flour
1 cup cornmeal

2 tsp. baking powder
½ tsp. salt
1½ cups buttermilk
1 cup cranberries, halved

Cream together the butter and sugar. Add eggs; mix well.
Combine the flour, cornmeal, baking powder, and salt. Add
to creamed mixture alternately with buttermilk. Fold in
cranberries. Transfer to a greased 9-inch square pan. Bake at
375° for 40–45 minutes or until toothpick inserted in center
comes out clean. Serve warm.

Note: Whole blueberries, coated in flour, can be used instead of
the cranberries.

Apricot Nut Bread

2½ cups flour
½ cup sugar
½ cup brown sugar
3½ tsp. baking powder
1 tsp. salt

3 T. vegetable oil
1¼ cups milk
1 egg
1 cup chopped nuts
1 cup finely cut-up dried
    apricots

Mix all ingredients; beat 30 seconds. Pour into 1 large loaf pan
or 2 medium loaf pans, greased. Bake at 350° for 55–65 minutes.
Cool slightly. Remove from pans and cool completely.

Healthy Apple-Walnut Muffins

2 cups flour
1 tsp. baking soda
¼ rounded tsp. salt
¼ tsp. cinnamon
¼ tsp. ginger
¼ tsp. allspice
¼ tsp. nutmeg
2 large eggs
1 cup plus 2 T. frozen apple
   juice concentrate, thawed

⅔ cup buttermilk
2 T. oat bran
2 small Granny Smith
   apples, peeled, cored, and
   chopped
⅓ cup chopped walnuts
1 small Granny Smith apple,
   peeled, cored, and cut into
   12 thin slices

Mix flour, baking soda, salt, and spices. Mix together eggs, apple juice, and buttermilk. Stir flour mixture and oat bran into egg mixture until dry ingredients are just moistened. Do not overmix. Gently stir in chopped apples and nuts. Spoon batter into 12 greased or paper-lined muffin pan cups. Garnish each muffin with an apple slice. Bake at 375° for 25 minutes or until tops spring back when pressed. Cool slightly; remove from pan.

SALADS
AND GELATIN
SALADS

Pineapple Gelatin Salad

First layer:
1 20-oz. can crushed
    pineapple
1 package (6 oz.) lemon
    flavored gelatin
3 cups boiling water

Second layer:
1 8-oz. package cream cheese,
    softened

1 16-oz. carton frozen
    whipped topping, thawed

Topping:
¾ cup sugar
3 T. lemon juice
3 T. water
reserved pineapple juice
2 egg yolks, lightly beaten
2 T. flour

For first layer: Drain pineapple, reserving juice. Dissolve gelatin in boiling water; add pineapple. Pour into a 13 x 9-inch pan and chill until almost set, about 45 minutes.

For second layer: Beat cream cheese and whipped topping until smooth. Carefully spread over gelatin and chill for 30 minutes.

For topping: Meanwhile, in a saucepan over medium heat, combine all topping ingredients. Bring to a boil, stirring constantly. Cook for 1 minute or until thickened. Cool. Carefully spread over cream cheese layer. Chill for at least 1 hour.

The lowest ebb is the turn of the tide.

Strawberry Lettuce Salad

½ cup Miracle Whip
¼ cup milk
¼ cup sugar
⅛ cup white vinegar
1 T. poppy seeds
1 head romaine lettuce, torn
    into bite-sized pieces

½ red onion, sliced
1 cup sliced fresh strawberries
½ cup toasted pecans
¼ cup red bell pepper,
    chopped

In small bowl, mix together Miracle Whip, milk, sugar. Add vinegar and poppy seeds. Refrigerate until ready to use. Combine lettuce, onion, strawberries, pecans, and red bell pepper in a salad bowl. Toss with dressing. Yummy!

Green Salad

1 24-oz. container cottage cheese
1 6-oz. package lime gelatin, dry
1 20-oz. can drained, crushed pineapple

2 handfuls miniature marshmallows
1 16-oz. container whipped topping

Stir the cottage cheese and gelatin and then add the rest of the ingredients; mix well. Refrigerate. This makes a large batch.

Lime Gelatin Salad

1 6-oz. package lime gelatin
1 cup boiling water
1 8-oz. package cream cheese, softened
½ tsp. vanilla
1 15-oz. can mandarin oranges, drained

1 8-oz. can crushed pineapple, drained
1 cup lemon-lime soda
½ cup chopped pecans
1 8-oz. container whipped topping

Dissolve gelatin in water. In mixing bowl, beat cream cheese until fluffy. Stir in gelatin mixture and beat until smooth. Stir in vanilla, oranges, pineapple, soda, and pecans. Chill until mixture mounds slightly when dropped with a spoon. Fold in whipped topping and pour into 13 x 9-inch pan. Chill until firm.

Loaded Baked Potato Salad

5 lbs. small unpeeled red
   potatoes, cubed
1 tsp. salt
½ tsp. pepper
8 hard-cooked eggs, chopped
1 lb. sliced bacon, cooked and
   crumbled
2 cups shredded Cheddar
   cheese

1 medium Vidalia or sweet
   onion, chopped
3 dill pickles, chopped
   (optional)
1½ cups (12 oz.) sour cream
1 cup mayonnaise
2 to 3 tsp. prepared mustard

Place the potatoes in a greased 15 x 10-inch baking pan; sprinkle with salt and pepper. Bake, uncovered, at 425° for 40–45 minutes or until tender. Cool in pan. In a large bowl, combine the potatoes, eggs, bacon, cheese, onion, and pickles. In a small bowl, combine sour cream, mayonnaise, and mustard; pour over potato mixture and toss to coat. Serve immediately.

A great deal of what we see depends on what we are looking for.

Seven Layer Salad

1 head lettuce, torn into bite-
   size pieces
1 onion, chopped
½ cup chopped celery
½ cup chopped green pepper
1 grated carrot

1½ cups frozen peas
8 slices bacon, cooked and
   crumbled
2 cups Miracle Whip
2 T. sugar
4 oz. shredded Cheddar
   cheese

Layer all ingredients in order given except last three in 13 x 9-inch pan. Mix Miracle Whip and sugar and spread on top and then sprinkle with cheese. Refrigerate overnight.

Southwestern Cobb Salad

2 packages (10 oz. each) mixed baby salad greens, about 10 cups
2 6-oz. packages southwestern seasoned chicken breast strips
4 hard-cooked eggs, chopped
1 16-oz. can black beans, drained and rinsed
1 cup shredded Mexican cheese blend
12 slices bacon, cooked and crumbled
2 small ripe avocados, peeled and sliced
2 cups halved cherry tomatoes
⅔ cup Ranch dressing
⅓ cup salsa
¼ tsp. cumin

Winning is not always success and losing is not always failure.

Arrange salad greens evenly on large serving platter. Arrange chicken, eggs, beans, cheese, bacon, avocados, and tomatoes in even rows on top of greens. Mix dressing, salsa, and cumin. Serve on the side. Serve immediately.

I usually make a double batch of dressing, and the cumin makes it even better.

Cauliflower Salad

1 head lettuce, cut into bite-sized pieces
1 head cauliflower, cut into small pieces
1 sweet onion, chopped
1 lb. bacon, cut into small pieces and fried
2 cups mayonnaise
½ cup sugar
½ cup Parmesan cheese

Layer in bowl in order given, mixing together mayonnaise and sugar before spreading on top of bacon. Refrigerate overnight. Toss before serving.

Apple Caesar Salad

¾ cup olive oil, divided
4 to 6 garlic cloves, peeled,
   divided
¾ tsp. salt, divided
6 cups cubed French bread
¼ cup lemon juice
1½ T. Dijon mustard

1½ tsp. Worcestershire sauce
½ tsp. pepper
12 cups torn romaine lettuce
⅓ cup shredded Parmesan
   cheese
3 medium apples or ripe
   pears, diced

For croutons, combine ¼ cup oil, 2–3 garlic cloves and ¼ teaspoon salt in a bowl; let stand for 1 hour. Strain oil and discard garlic. Toss bread cubes in the oil; place on a baking sheet. Bake at 400° for 7–9 minutes or until golden brown, stirring occasionally. Cool.

In a small bowl, combine the lemon juice, mustard, Worcestershire sauce, pepper, and remaining oil and salt. Mince remaining garlic; stir into dressing. Place romaine in a salad bowl; drizzle with dressing. Add the croutons, Parmesan cheese, and apple; toss to coat.

Overnight Fruit Cup

1 3-oz. package lemon gelatin
2 cups boiling water
1 6-oz. can frozen orange juice
   concentrate, thawed
1 20-oz. can pineapple
   chunks, undrained
1 15¼-oz. can sliced peaches,
   drained

1 11-oz. can mandarin
   oranges, undrained
1 cup sliced fresh strawberries
1 cup fresh blueberries
1 cup green grapes
1 firm banana, thinly sliced

In a large bowl, dissolve gelatin in water. Add orange juice concentrate; mix well. Add all the fruit; mix well. Cover and refrigerate overnight.

Fruit Salad

1 medium honeydew, peeled, seeded, and cubed

1 medium cantaloupe, peeled, seeded, and cubed

2 cups cubed seedless watermelon

2 medium peaches, peeled and sliced

2 medium nectarines, sliced

1 cup seedless red grapes

1 cup fresh strawberries, halved

1 11-oz. can mandarin oranges, drained

2 kiwis, peeled, halved, and sliced

2 medium firm bananas, sliced

1 large Granny Smith apple, cubed

1 12-oz. can frozen lemonade concentrate, thawed

1 3.4-oz. package instant vanilla pudding

Combine the first nine ingredients in a large bowl and refrigerate until ready to serve, at least 1 hour. Just before serving, slice in bananas and apples. Combine lemonade concentrate and pudding mix. Pour over fruit and toss gently to coat.

Applesauce Berry Gelatin

2 packages (3 oz. each) strawberry gelatin

2 cups boiling water

1 16-oz. can whole berry cranberry sauce

1¾ cups chunky applesauce

Dissolve gelatin in boiling water. Stir in cranberry sauce and applesauce. Pour into 6-cup ring mold coated with nonstick cooking spray. Cover and refrigerate overnight. Unmold onto a serving platter.

Cranberry Salad

2 packages (3 oz. each)
    raspberry gelatin
2 cups boiling water
1 20-oz. can crushed
    pineapple, undrained

1 can whole berry cranberry
    sauce
½ cup English walnuts or
    pecans

Dissolve gelatin in water. Add pineapple, cranberry sauce, and nuts. Pour into glass serving dish and refrigerate until set.

Seven Layer Gelatin Salad

2 packages unflavored gelatin
2 cups milk
1 cup sugar
16 oz. sour cream
1 tsp. vanilla
1 3-oz. package lime gelatin

1 3-oz. package lemon gelatin
1 3-oz. package cherry gelatin
1 3-oz. package orange gelatin
boiling water
cold water

Soften unflavored gelatin in ½ cup cold water. Bring milk to a boil and stir in gelatin to dissolve. Remove from heat and stir in sugar, sour cream, and vanilla. Set aside.

One box at a time, dissolve 1 box flavored gelatin in 1 cup boiling water. Stir in ½ cup cold water and pour into 13 x 9-inch pan. Chill in refrigerator until set. Pour on 1½ cups sour cream mixture and let set again. Alternate until all of the gelatin and all of the sour cream mixture is used. When adding a layer, pour over a spoon so it doesn't make a hole in the set layer. Do not cover pan while cooling.

In the midst of great anger do not answer a man's letter.

Creamy Coleslaw

cabbage, shredded (maybe ½ head or so)
1 carrot, shredded
apple
nuts
raisins

pineapple
4 tsp. mayonnaise
2 tsp. sugar
1 tsp. vinegar
½ cup cream or milk
salt to taste

Shred the cabbage and carrot. You can add any combination of fruits or nuts. For dressing, mix together the mayonnaise, sugar, and vinegar. Then add cream and salt (if desired) and pour over slaw.

Favorite Broccoli Salad

1 bunch broccoli, separated into florets
1 head cauliflower, separated into florets
8 bacon strips, cooked and crumbled
⅓ cup onion, chopped

1 cup seeded tomatoes, chopped
2 hard-cooked eggs, sliced
1 cup mayonnaise
⅓ cup sugar
2 T. vinegar

In a large bowl, combine broccoli, cauliflower, bacon, onion, tomatoes, and eggs; set aside. Mix mayonnaise, sugar, and vinegar. Just before serving, pour dressing over salad and toss. Yield: 6–8 servings.

Macaroni Salad

1 lb. box macaroni, cooked
   and drained
1 dozen hard-boiled eggs,
   diced
1 pint mayonnaise
1 T. prepared mustard
1 small onion, chopped
grated carrots, optional

Dressing:
2 cups sugar
¾ cup vinegar
4 eggs, beaten
½ tsp. salt
1 tsp. butter

For dressing, combine sugar, vinegar, eggs, salt, and butter. Cook until thickened; cool. When cool, pour over macaroni, eggs, mayonnaise, mustard, onion, and carrots; stir.

In the midst of great joy do not promise a man anything.

Mamm's Potato Salad

2 heaping quarts shoestring
   potatoes, cooked in jackets
   and peeled
9 hard-boiled eggs, chopped
1½ cups celery, diced
small onion, diced

Dressing:
2 T. mustard
1 T. salt
2 cups Miracle Whip
3 T. vinegar
⅓ cup milk
1⅓ cups sugar

Put potatoes, eggs, celery, and onion in large bowl. Mix dressing ingredients and pour over ingredients in bowl. Toss gently to combine and refrigerate until ready to use.

Fresh Apple Salad

¼ cup butter
¼ cup sugar
1 T. lemon juice
2 T. cornstarch or Clear Jel
2 T. water
1 cup mayonnaise

½ cup plain yogurt
8 cups chopped unpeeled, tart red apples
1 20-oz. can pineapple tidbits (reserve juice)
2 cups seedless green grapes
1½ cups pecans, toasted

Combine reserved pineapple juice, butter, sugar, and lemon juice in a small saucepan. Heat to boiling. Combine cornstarch and water to make a smooth paste. Add to hot mixture. Cook until thick and smooth. Chill completely before stirring in mayonnaise and yogurt.

Combine apples, pineapple, and grapes in a large bowl. Add chilled dressing. Refrigerate until ready to serve. Stir in pecans just before serving. Yield: 16 servings.

Cabbage Salad

1 head cabbage, shredded
3 tomatoes, chopped
1 onion, finely chopped
1 pepper, chopped
½ lb. Monterey Jack cheese, cubed
2 carrots, grated

Dressing:
⅔ cup vinegar
⅔ cup sugar
2 tsp. celery seed
1 tsp. salt
¼ tsp. pepper
⅔ cup oil

For dressing: In a saucepan, combine all dressing ingredients except the oil and bring to a boil. Remove from heat and then add oil. Mix dressing with all other ingredients and let marinate at least 2 hours before serving.

Caesar Salad Croutons

¼ cup Parmesan cheese
½ tsp. oregano
½ tsp. celery salt

½ tsp. garlic salt
¼ cup oil
8 slices bread, cubed ¾ inch

Mix cheese, oregano, celery salt, garlic salt, and oil. Toss with bread cubes. Place on a cookie sheet and bake at 275° until crispy, about 45 minutes, stirring every 15 minutes. If not crispy enough bake a bit longer.

Norma's Pasta Salad with Mexican Dressing

12 oz. tricolor spiral pasta,
   boiled according to
   package directions
1 onion, chopped
1 cup chopped cooked ham
1 cup Cheddar cheese, cubed
1 16-oz. can red kidney beans,
   drained and rinsed
4 hard-boiled eggs, chopped

Mexican Dressing:
1 large onion, chopped
1½ cups sugar
1½ tsp. salt
¾ tsp. pepper
1½ tsp. celery seed
½ cup vinegar
1½ cups oil
6 T. mayonnaise
1½ T. prepared mustard

Combine all dressing ingredients; blend well and store in refrigerator. Mix together the salad ingredients and toss with Mexican Dressing. It's good if left to sit a while before serving.

Easy Caesar Salad

⅓ cup plus 2 T. olive oil
½ tsp. salt
1 large clove garlic
2 tomatoes, cut in eighths
2 heads romaine lettuce, cut in 1-inch strips
¼ cup chopped green onions
½ cup grated Romano cheese

1 lb. bacon, fried and crumbled
juice of 2 medium lemons or 6 T. lemon juice
½ tsp. pepper
½ tsp. oregano
1 lightly soft-boiled egg
1 cup croutons

Pour 2 tablespoons oil into a large wooden bowl. Sprinkle with salt and rub with a clove of garlic. Place tomatoes in bowl. Add romaine lettuce, onions, cheese, and bacon. Mix ⅓ cup oil, lemon juice, pepper, and oregano. Add egg and whisk vigorously. Pour dressing over salad when ready to serve. Add croutons. Toss and serve.

Asian Salad

1 16-oz. package broccoli slaw
1 diced red pepper
1 cup sunflower kernels
1 cup slivered almonds
2 packages chicken-flavored ramen noodles, crushed
2 T. butter
4 green onions, chopped

Dressing:
1 cup canola oil
½ cup sugar
⅓ cup red wine vinegar
2 packets seasoning from Ramen noodles

Mix together all dressing ingredients and set aside. Toast the sunflower kernels, almonds, and noodles (packets of seasoning removed) in butter in skillet until golden. Watch closely. Remove from heat and cool. Mix together salad ingredients. Just before serving add dressing.

Taco Salad

2 lbs. hamburger
1 onion, chopped
8 oz. Velveeta cheese
8 oz. Thousand Island
   dressing
1 tsp. hot sauce

¾ tsp. salt
1 can kidney beans, drained
lettuce
tomatoes
nacho cheese chips, broken
   into small pieces

Fry hamburger and onion. Drain. Add cheese, dressing, hot
sauce, salt, and kidney beans. Serve with lettuce, tomatoes, and
chips.

*Sign on a
buggy: "The
original
green energy
with the
original
odor."*

SOUPS
AND
SANDWICHES

Cheesy Potato Soup

½ cup butter, melted
1 medium onion, chopped
1 celery rib, chopped
1 medium carrot, grated
2 T. flour
4 cups milk
1 can condensed cream of
    mushroom soup

½ cup Cheddar cheese,
    shredded
6 large potatoes, peeled,
    diced, and cooked in salt
    water
1 tsp. seasoned salt

Sauté onion, celery, and carrot in butter. Stir flour in until
blended. Gradually add milk. Cook and stir for 2 minutes or
until thickened. Add soup, cheese, potatoes, and seasoned salt.
Cook and stir until cheese is melted and soup is heated through.
Yield: 10–12 servings.

Miriam's Chili

3 lbs. ground hamburger
1 medium onion, chopped
5 quarts tomato juice
2 43-oz. cans pork and beans
1 tsp. chili powder
2–4 T. flour

1 cup brown sugar
1 T. salt
1 1.5-oz. packet chili seasoning
dash of black pepper
4 cans tomato soup

Fry hamburger and onions together; drain. Add remaining
ingredients and heat through. Note: You can use a combination
of pork and beans and kidney beans instead of just pork and
beans. This makes a *big* batch.

Ella's Broccoli Soup

From *Ella's Wish*

"Why don't I eat a little with you?" he said, laying his hat on the floor. "I had supper, but your soup looks good. I have to see how you cook, now, don't I?" He laughed softly.

2 cups chopped broccoli
½ tsp. onion flakes
¼ cup carrots
1 cup celery
2 cups chicken broth
2¼ cups chicken

1 cup milk
1 8-oz. can evaporated milk
1 can cream of celery or
   chicken soup
salt and pepper
Velveeta cheese

Love has reasons which reason fails to recognize.

Cook broccoli, onion flakes, carrots, celery, and broth 7–10 minutes. Add chicken, milks, soup, and salt and pepper to taste. Continue cooking for 10 minutes. Add cheese to taste.

White Chili

4 cups boneless chicken
   breast, cut into small
   pieces
1 or 2 onions, chopped
2 cloves garlic, chopped
1 T. oil
3 cans chicken broth
3 cans Great Northern beans,
   rinsed and drained

1 can diced tomatoes with
   green chilies
2 tsp. cumin
½ tsp. oregano
¼–½ tsp. celery salt
Monterey Jack cheese

Cook the chicken, onion, and garlic in the oil. Add broth and simmer about 10 minutes. Add all remaining ingredients and simmer 5 or 10 minutes longer. Serve with Monterey Jack cheese.

Lasagna Soup

1 lb. lean ground beef
1 large green pepper, chopped
1 medium onion, chopped
2 garlic cloves, minced
2 cans (14½ oz. each) beef
  broth
2 cans (14½ oz. each) diced
  tomatoes
1 8-oz. can tomato sauce

1 cup frozen corn
¼ cup tomato paste
2 tsp. Italian seasoning
¼ tsp. pepper
2½ cups uncooked spiral
  pasta
½ cup shredded Parmesan
  cheese

In large saucepan, cook the beef, green pepper, and onion until meat is no longer pink. Add garlic; cook 1 minute longer. Drain. Stir in the broth, tomatoes, tomato sauce, corn, tomato paste, Italian seasoning, and pepper. Bring to a boil. Stir in pasta. Return to a boil. Reduce heat; cover and simmer for 10–12 minutes or until pasta is tender. Sprinkle with cheese and serve.

Daett's Favorite Rivel Soup

3 T. butter
1 quart milk
salt to taste

Rivels:
1½ cups flour
1 large egg, beaten with fork
celery salt, if desired

Butter can be melted and browned if desired. Add milk and salt. Heat to almost boiling.

Mix flour and egg to make rivels or clumps; add bits of dough to milk and bring to a boil. (All of these amounts are approximate as Mom never measured for this soup.) Sprinkle with celery salt when ready to eat if desired. Serve with crackers. Pickles and pickled red beets are good with this too.

Salmon Chowder

3 T. butter
1 onion, diced
3 T. flour
½ tsp. salt
⅛ tsp. pepper

2 cups boiling water
3 medium potatoes, peeled
 and diced
1 8-oz. can salmon
2 cups milk

Melt butter. Add onions and sauté until soft. Stir in flour and seasonings; add the boiling water and potatoes. Simmer until the potatoes are tender (about 15 minutes). Remove the skin and bones from the salmon; add to the soup together with the milk. Bring just to boiling point.

Grilled Ham and Egg Salad Sandwiches

6 hard-cooked eggs, chopped
1 cup diced fully cooked ham
½ cup finely chopped celery
½ cup mayonnaise
2 tsp. prepared mustard
1 T. minced onion, dried
½ tsp. salt
¼ tsp. pepper

12 slices bread
oil for frying
½ cup cornmeal
½ cup flour
1 tsp. salt
1 tsp. baking powder
2 cups milk
2 eggs, lightly beaten

Combine first eight ingredients. Place on six slices of bread; top with six other slices. Whisk together last six ingredients. Heat about a half-inch of oil in a large deep skillet. Dip sandwiches in batter. Fry in hot oil for 3 minutes or until golden brown on both sides. Drain on paper towels.

Baked Southwest Sandwiches

1 4¼-oz. can chopped ripe olives, drained
½ tsp. chili powder
½ tsp. ground cumin
¼ tsp. salt
½ cup mayonnaise
⅓ cup chopped green onions
⅓ cup sour cream
8 slices Italian bread

¾ to 1 lb. thinly sliced cooked turkey
2 medium tomatoes, thinly sliced
2 ripe avocados, peeled and sliced
¾ cup Cheddar cheese, shredded
¾ cup Monterey Jack cheese, shredded

Combine olives, chili powder, cumin, and salt. Set aside 2 tablespoons. Add mayonnaise, green onions, and sour cream to the remaining olive mixture. Place bread on ungreased cookie sheet. Spread 1 tablespoon of mayonnaise mixture on each slice. Top with turkey and tomatoes. Spread with another tablespoon of mayonnaise mixture. Top with avocados and cheeses. Sprinkle with reserved olive mixture. Bake at 350° for 15 minutes, or until heated through. Makes 8 servings.

Man is still the master of the unspoken word.

Egg Salad Sandwiches

6 hard-cooked eggs, chopped
½ cup chopped celery
⅓ cup mayonnaise

¼ tsp. salt
dash of pepper
1 T. finely chopped onion or dried minced onion

Mix together all ingredients. Spread over bread to make sandwiches. Note: may add chopped ham.

Chicken Salad Sandwiches

1½ cups cooked chicken,
    chopped
½ cup celery, chopped
1 T. onion, chopped
1 8-oz. package cream cheese,
    softened

½ cup mayonnaise
½ tsp. onion powder
½ tsp. salt

Mix together all ingredients. Make sandwiches. Yield: about 2½ cups, enough for at least six sandwiches. This can also be used as a dip for crackers if blended in the blender.

Shredded Venison Sandwiches

1 boneless venison roast,
    about 4 pounds
1½ cups ketchup
3 T. brown sugar
1 T. ground mustard
1 T. lemon juice
1 T. soy sauce

1 T. liquid smoke
2 tsp. celery salt
2 tsp. pepper
2 tsp. Worcestershire sauce
1 tsp. onion powder
1 tsp. garlic powder
3 drops hot pepper sauce

Cut venison roast in half; place in 5-quart slow cooker. Combine the rest of the ingredients and pour over roast. Cover and cook on high for 4–5 hours or until tender. Remove the roast and strain the sauce. Return the sauce to cooker and shred the roast using two forks. Return to cooker; heat through. Serve on hamburger buns.

Sloppy Joes

2½ lbs. hamburger
1 medium onion, chopped
salt, pepper, and garlic
    powder
½ cup ketchup
⅓ cup brown sugar
2½ T. Worcestershire sauce
1 T. prepared mustard
1 can cream of mushroom
    soup

Fry hamburger and onion; drain. Season with salt, pepper, and garlic powder. Add the rest of the ingredients. Heat and serve on warm buns.

Baked Venison Burgers

¾ cup quick-cooking oats
¾ cup milk
¼ cup chopped onion
1 egg, beaten
½ to 1 tsp. seasoned salt
1 lb. ground venison
1 lb. ground beef
⅓ cup ketchup
1 T. brown sugar
1 T. Worcestershire sauce
1 T. prepared mustard

Combine first five ingredients. Mix with venison and beef. Mix well. Shape into eight patties; place in a greased 15 x 10-inch cookie sheet. Mix the rest of the ingredients and spoon over patties. Bake at 350° for 22–26 minutes or until meat juices run clear. Serve on rolls with Swiss cheese and tomato slices. Very good and moist.

If the grass looks greener on the other side of the fence, perhaps they take better care of it there.

Hot Ham and Cheese Slices

1 cup sliced fresh mushrooms
1 small sweet red pepper, chopped
2 green onions, chopped
2 T. butter

1 17.3-oz. package frozen puff pastry, thawed
½ lb. thinly sliced deli ham
½ lb. sliced Swiss cheese

In a large skillet, sauté the mushrooms, pepper, and onions in butter until tender. Set aside. Unfold pastry. Layer the ham, cheese, and mushroom mixture off-center on each sheet of pastry. Fold pastry over filling; pinch seams to seal. Place in a greased 15 x 10-inch baking pan. Bake at 400° for 18–22 minutes or until golden brown. Let stand for 5 minutes. Cut each with a serrated knife into 4 slices.

You shouldn't worry if you don't know all the answers— you probably won't be asked all the questions.

Pork BBQ Sandwiches

1 bone-in pork shoulder roast, about 4 lbs.
1 cup water
1 tsp. salt
2 cups finely chopped celery
⅓ cup steak sauce
¼ cup brown sugar
¼ cup cider vinegar

2 tsp. lemon juice
2 tsp. chili sauce
1 tsp. ketchup
2 medium onions, sliced
2 tsp. sugar
1 T. olive oil
1 T. butter
16 hoagie buns, split

In a Dutch oven, bring the pork roast, water, and salt to a boil. Reduce heat; cover and simmer for 3½–4 hours or until the meat is very tender. Remove meat and let stand until cool enough to handle. Discard bone; shred meat with two forks. Skim fat from pan juices. Stir in the celery, steak sauce, brown sugar, vinegar, lemon juice, chili sauce, ketchup, and shredded pork. Bring to a boil. Reduce heat; cover and simmer for 1 hour. In large skillet, cook onions and sugar in oil and butter over low heat for 20–30 minutes or until golden brown and tender, stirring occasionally. Serve pork and onions on buns.

Creamed Cabbage Soup

2 T. olive oil

1 medium onion, chopped

2 celery ribs, chopped

1 medium carrot, chopped

1 tsp. thyme

1 medium head cabbage, shredded (about 3 lbs.)

2 cans (14½ oz. each) chicken broth

¼ cup butter

3 T. flour

1 tsp. salt

¼ tsp. pepper

2 cups half-and-half cream

1 cup milk

2 cups cubed fully cooked ham

Heat olive oil in a Dutch oven until shimmering. Add onion, celery, carrots, and thyme and cook, stirring, until just tender. Stir in cabbage and cook 1 minute longer. Pour in broth. Bring to a boil, then reduce heat and cover. Let simmer 15 minutes. Meanwhile, melt butter in saucepan. Add the flour, salt, and pepper; stir to form a smooth paste. Combine cream and milk; gradually add to flour mixture, stirring constantly. Cook and stir until thickened; continue cooking 1 minute longer. Gradually stir into soup. Add the ham and heat through.

Cheesy Chicken Chowder

2 T. olive oil
½ cup diced onion
1 cup diced celery
1 cup diced carrots
2 cups diced, peeled potatoes
3 cups chicken broth
1½ tsp. salt

¼ tsp. pepper
¼ cup butter
⅓ cup flour
2 cups milk
2 cups (8 oz.) shredded
   Cheddar cheese
2 cups diced cooked chicken

Heat oil in Dutch oven until shimmering. Add onion, celery, carrots, and potatoes and cook, stirring, about 5 minutes. Add broth, salt, and pepper. Bring to a boil, then reduce heat and cover. Let simmer 20 minutes or until potatoes are tender. Meanwhile, melt butter. Add flour and mix well. Gradually stir in milk; cook over low heat until slightly thickened. Stir in cheese and cook until melted; add to broth along with chicken. Cook and stir over low heat until heated through. Yield: 6–8 servings.

Chicken Salad Wraps

2 lbs. chicken breast, diced
oil
1 cup Ranch dressing
1 package fajita seasoning
1 stalk celery, diced

¼ cup chopped green pepper
2 T. chopped onion
½ cup shredded Cheddar
   cheese
10 tortillas, warmed

Stir-fry chicken breast in oil until chicken is done. Remove chicken and add Ranch dressing, seasoning, celery, green pepper, onion, and cheese. Divide among the 10 tortillas. Wrap and serve.

Ultimate Grilled Cheese Sandwiches

3 oz. cream cheese, softened
¾ cup mayonnaise
1 cup shredded Cheddar
  cheese
1 cup shredded mozzarella
  cheese

½ tsp. garlic powder
⅛ tsp. seasoning salt
10 slices bread, buttered on
  one side

Beat cream cheese and mayonnaise until smooth. Stir in cheeses and seasonings. Spread onto bread, top sandwich with another buttered piece of bread, and grill, buttered side out, on a frying pan. Yield: 5 servings.

You never get a second chance to make a first impression.

Ham Stromboli

1 11-oz. tube refrigerated
  crusty French loaf
4 slices American cheese
¼ lb. deli ham, thinly sliced

1 cup shredded Cheddar
  cheese
1 T. butter, melted
1 T. grated Parmesan cheese

Unroll dough at seam. Pat dough into a 12 x 14-inch rectangle. Place American cheese, ham, and Cheddar cheese on dough. Roll up tightly from short side; pinch seam side down on a 10 x 15-inch baking sheet. Brush top of loaf with butter; sprinkle with Parmesan cheese. Bake at 375° for 20 minutes or until golden brown. Yield: 4–5 servings.

Bert and Leona Weaver were out on a
Sunday afternoon drive visiting relatives.
Before leaving the house, Bert had insisted
he wear one of his work shirts, over Leona's
strenuous objections. He then made things
worse by wearing his work shoes.
Silence had settled in the buggy, and
passing a barnyard filled with mules and
pigs, Leona motioned with her bonnet,
"Might those be relatives of yours?"
"Ya," Bert said. "They look like in-laws."

VEGETABLES
AND
SIDE DISHES

Sweet Potatoes with Apples

3 to 3½ lbs. sweet potatoes
2 tart apples
½ cup orange juice
¼ cup brown sugar

¼ tsp. cinnamon
¼ tsp. ginger
2 tsp. butter

Put sweet potatoes in a large saucepan; cover with water and bring to a boil. Reduce heat, cover, and let simmer for 30 minutes or until just tender. Drain and cool slightly. Peel and cut into ¼-inch slices. Peel and core apples and cut into ¼-inch rings. Alternate layers of potatoes and apples in a greased 13 x 9-inch pan. Pour orange juice over potatoes and apples. Mix together the brown sugar and spices and sprinkle over orange juice. Dot with butter. Bake, uncovered, at 350° for 35–45 minutes or until apples are tender.

Old-Fashioned Green Beans

6 bacon strips, cut in ½-inch
    pieces
2 lbs. fresh green beans

3 tsp. brown sugar
½ cup water

Cook bacon until crisp and tender. Add the rest of the ingredients. Stir gently. Bring to a boil. Cover and simmer for 15 minutes or until beans are crisp and tender.

Every great person has first learned to obey, whom to obey, and when to obey.

Make-Ahead Mashed Potatoes

10 large potatoes, peeled and
    quartered
6 T. butter, divided
1 8-oz. package cream cheese

1 cup sour cream
2 T. dried minced onion
1 tsp. salt
paprika

Cook potatoes till tender; drain. Add to potatoes 4 tablespoons butter and the cream cheese. Beat until smooth. Add sour cream, onion, and salt. Taste to make sure it has enough salt. Spread in a greased 13 x 9-inch pan. Melt remaining butter and drizzle over potatoes. Sprinkle with paprika. Refrigerate or bake immediately at 350° for 40 minutes; uncover and bake 20 minutes more. If potatoes are made ahead and refrigerated, let stand at room temperature for 30 minutes before baking.

Harvest Potatoes

4 cups peeled, cubed or
    grated, and cooked
    potatoes
1 can cream of chicken soup
½ cup butter, melted
1½ tsp. salt

1 medium onion, chopped
1 cup sour cream
2 cups shredded Cheddar
    cheese
1 cup crushed cornflakes or
    chips

Combine potatoes, soup, butter, salt, onion, sour cream, and cheese. Pour into greased 9 x 13-inch pan. Top with cornflakes or chips. Bake at 350° for one hour. Cooked ham or browned sausage slices may be added.

Variation: Sometimes I put in more potatoes and use sharp Cheddar cheese. Also, I often omit the onion.

Creamy Scalloped Potatoes

2 lbs. potatoes (about 6
  medium)
4 T. butter, divided
3 T. flour
1 tsp. salt

¼ tsp. pepper
2½ cups milk
1 small onion, finely chopped
  (about ¼ cup)

Peel potatoes and slice very thin. Melt 3 tablespoons butter. Blend in flour, salt, and pepper. Cook and stir until smooth and bubbly. Stir in milk. Heat to boiling, stirring constantly. Boil and stir 1 minute. Arrange potatoes in greased two-quart casserole in three layers, topping each of the first two layers with half of the onion and a third of the sauce. Top with remaining potatoes and sauce. Dot with 1 tablespoon butter. Cover and cook at 325° for 40 minutes. Uncover and cook at 350° for 60 to 70 minutes or until potatoes are tender. Let stand 5 to 10 minutes before serving.

Butternut Squash Bake

⅓ cup butter, softened
¾ cup sugar
2 eggs
1 5-oz. can evaporated milk
1 tsp. vanilla
2 cups mashed, cooked
  butternut squash

Topping:
½ cup rice cereal
¼ cup brown sugar
¼ cup chopped pecans
2 tsp. butter, melted

Preheat oven to 350°. Grease an 11 x 7-inch baking pan. Cream butter and sugar. Beat in eggs, evaporated milk, and vanilla. Stir in squash. Pour into pan. Bake 45 minutes or until almost set. For topping, combine cereal, brown sugar, pecans, and butter. Sprinkle on top. Bake 5–10 minutes longer or until bubbly.

Farmer's Potatoes

3 lbs. potatoes (about 9 medium), peeled and cubed

1 8-oz. package cream cheese, softened

½ cup sour cream

½ cup butter

¼ cup milk

1½ tsp. onion powder

1 tsp. salt

1 tsp. garlic powder

½ tsp. pepper

6 bacon strips, chopped

1 cup (4 oz.) shredded Cheddar cheese

3 green onions, chopped

Cook potatoes until tender. Drain; mash potatoes with cream cheese, sour cream, and butter. Stir in milk and seasonings. In small skillet, cook bacon until crisp. Drain on paper towels. Transfer potato mixture to greased 13 x 9-inch baking dish. Sprinkle with cheese, onions, and bacon. Cover and refrigerate until ready to use. Remove from refrigerator 30 minutes before baking. Bake uncovered at 350° for 40–50 minutes or until heated through.

We aren't really perfect, we're just blind to our own faults.

Baked Vegetable Medley

1 medium head cauliflower, cut into florets

1 bunch broccoli, cut into florets

6 medium carrots, sliced

1 lb. sliced, fresh mushrooms

1 bunch green onion, sliced

(I put in much less)

¼ cup butter, melted

1 can cream of chicken soup

½ cup milk

½ cup process cheese sauce

salt and seasoned salt to taste, optional

Place cauliflower, broccoli, and carrots in saucepan with 1 inch water in the bottom. Boil 7–9 minutes, until crisp-tender. In large skillet, sauté mushrooms and onions in butter until tender.

Drain vegetables. In large bowl, combine soup, milk, and cheese. Add vegetables and mushroom mixture and salts if desired. Toss to coat. Put into greased two-quart casserole. Cover and refrigerate overnight. Remove from refrigerator 30 minutes before baking. Bake uncovered at 350° for 40–50 minutes or until bubbly.

Green Beans Supreme

4 16-oz. packages frozen cut green beans
¼ cup finely chopped onion
¼ cup butter, cubed
2 tsp. flour
1 tsp. salt
1 tsp. paprika

1 tsp. Worcestershire sauce
½ tsp. ground mustard
2 8-oz. cans evaporated milk
8 oz. process cheese, shredded

Topping:
¼ cup dry bread crumbs
2 tsp. butter, melted

Boil green beans in large pot for 4–6 minutes until crisp-tender. In a Dutch oven, sauté onion in butter until tender. Remove from heat; whisk in flour, salt, paprika, Worcestershire sauce, and mustard until blended. Gradually stir in evaporated milk. Bring to a boil; cook and stir for 2 minutes or until thickened and bubbly. Remove from the heat; stir in cheese. Drain beans; gently fold into cheese sauce. Transfer to a large serving bowl. Toss bread crumbs and butter; sprinkle over beans.

Caramel Sweet Potatoes

5 medium sweet potatoes
¼ cup cream
1 tsp. salt
1 cup brown sugar

1 T. flour
2 tsp. butter
8 marshmallows

Boil sweet potatoes until just tender. Peel and cut in half lengthwise. Arrange in greased baking dish. Mix together the salt, brown sugar, and flour. Sprinkle over potatoes and dot with butter. Add marshmallows and pour cream over all. Bake at 350° for 40–45 minutes.

Country Green Beans

1 lb. fresh green beans,
   trimmed
¼ cup chopped onion
¼ cup chopped fully cooked
   ham

¼ cup butter
¼ cup water
1 garlic clove, minced
½ tsp. salt
¼ tsp. pepper

In a saucepan, combine all ingredients. Cover and simmer for 15–20 minutes or until beans are tender. Yield 4 servings.

Potluck Potato Casserole

2 lbs. potatoes, boiled in
jackets and then peeled
and chopped
8 T. melted butter, divided
1 tsp. salt
¼ tsp. pepper

½ cup chopped onion
1 can cream of chicken soup
1 pint sour cream
2 cups grated sharp Cheddar
cheese
2 cups crushed cornflakes

Combine potatoes and 4 tablespoons butter in a large mixing
bowl. Add salt, pepper, onion, soup, sour cream, and cheese.
Blend thoroughly. Pour into a greased 13 x 9-inch pan. Mix
cornflakes and the rest of the butter; put on top of potato
mixture. Bake at 350° for 45 minutes or until done.

*Before we
speak we
should
think twice
or perhaps
keep on
thinking.*

Roasted Green Beans

¾ lb. fresh green beans
1 small onion, thinly sliced
and separated into rings

2 garlic cloves, thinly sliced
1 T. red wine vinegar
2 tsp. olive oil

Place beans in a saucepan and cover with water; bring to a boil.
Cook uncovered for 8–10 minutes or until crisp-tender. Drain.
Place beans in a greased 11 x 7-inch pan. Top with onion and
garlic. Drizzle with vinegar and oil; toss to coat. Bake uncovered
at 450° for 5 minutes. Stir; bake 5 minutes longer.

Spanish Rice

⅓ cup vegetable or canola oil
1½ cups uncooked rice
2 medium onions, finely chopped
1 medium green pepper, finely chopped
2 medium celery stalks, finely chopped
1 20-oz. can crushed tomatoes, undrained
2 tsp. cumin
2 tsp. garlic powder
1 tsp. salt
2 cans (14 oz. each) chicken broth
green onions, chopped, optional

Heat oil in a Dutch oven over medium-high heat. Add rice and cook until golden, about 3 minutes, stirring constantly. Add onions, bell pepper, celery, tomatoes, cumin, garlic powder, salt, and 1 can chicken broth. Bring to a boil, reduce heat, cover tightly, and simmer 20 minutes, or until liquid is absorbed. Add remaining can of broth; mix well and simmer 10 additional minutes. Garnish with green onion if desired.

Amish Sweet Rice

3 quarts boiling water
1 lb. long-grain white rice
2 eggs, beaten
1 cup white sugar
½ cup milk
1 tsp. vanilla
cinnamon

Add rice to boiling water and simmer without a lid for 1 hour. Pour off any water that has not been absorbed. Beat eggs, then stir in sugar and milk. Add a little of the hot rice, then pour egg mixture into rice and stir well. Add vanilla. Pour into a dish and sprinkle with cinnamon. Leftover rice can be mixed with whipped cream and eaten as a dessert.

Honduran Rice

3 T. oil
2 cups rice
½ tsp. minced garlic
½ medium onion, chopped
    fine
½ cup chopped tomato

3 cups boiling water
3 chicken bouillon cubes
1 tsp. salt
¼ tsp. garlic powder
¼ tsp. cilantro

Fry rice, garlic, onion, and tomato in oil over medium-high heat for 10 minutes. Carefully add the boiling water, bouillon, and seasonings. Stir well. Tilt the lid on pan to vent, and cook on medium heat until water is absorbed, about 20 minutes. Do not stir while cooking. Serve with Honduras beans, sour cream, and tortillas. Yield: 6–8 servings.

Maybe you don't have everything you want, but neither do you have everything you don't want.

Garlic Mashed Potatoes

5 lbs. unpeeled red potatoes,
    quartered
13 oz. (26 T.) butter, softened
5 oz. Romano cheese, grated

¼ cup plus 2 tsp. garlic,
    minced
2½ tsp. salt
2½ tsp. dried oregano

Bring a large pot of salted water to a boil. Add potatoes; cook until tender but still firm (approximately 45 minutes), and drain. Stir in butter, cheese, garlic, salt, and oregano. Mash with a potato masher or an electric mixer. Yield: 10 servings.

Broccoli Cheese Casserole

2 eggs, lightly beaten
1 can cream of mushroom
  soup
1 medium onion, chopped
1 cup shredded Cheddar
  cheese
1 cup shredded Swiss cheese

½ cup mayonnaise
2 T. butter, melted
1 16-oz. package frozen
  broccoli cuts, thawed
1 16-oz. package frozen
  chopped broccoli, thawed
¼ cup dry bread crumbs

Combine the first seven ingredients; fold in broccoli. Transfer to a greased 1½-quart baking dish. Sprinkle with bread crumbs. Cover and bake at 400° for 30–35 minutes or until heated through. Yield: 8 servings.

Twice-Baked Potato Cubes

6 medium unpeeled potatoes,
  baked
1 lb. bacon, cooked and
  crumbled
¼ tsp. salt
¼ tsp. pepper

3 cups sour cream
2 cups (8 oz.) shredded
  mozzarella cheese
2 cups (8 oz.) shredded
  Cheddar cheese
2 green onions, chopped

Cut baked potatoes into 1-inch cubes. Place half in a greased 13 x 9-inch pan. Sprinkle with bacon, salt, and pepper. Top with half of the sour cream and cheeses. Add onions. Repeat layers. Bake uncovered at 350° for 45 minutes.

Angel Hair Alfredo

8–12 oz. angel hair pasta
2 garlic cloves, minced
2 T. olive oil
1 T. flour
¼ tsp. garlic salt

¼ tsp. pepper
¼ tsp. basil
1½ cups milk
4 oz. cream cheese, cubed
¼ cup grated Parmesan
   cheese

Cook pasta according to package directions. Meanwhile, in a large skillet, sauté garlic in oil until lightly browned. Stir in flour, garlic salt, pepper, and basil until blended. Gradually stir in milk. Bring to a boil; cook and stir for 2 minutes or until thickened. Reduce heat; whisk in cream cheese and Parmesan cheese until smooth. Drain pasta; add to sauce and toss to coat. Very good served with chicken. Yield: 4–6 servings.

Spunky Baked Beans

1 lb. bacon
2 small onions, chopped
8 cans pork and beans (6
   drained and 2 undrained)
1 cup brown sugar

heaping ¼ cup honey
   barbecue sauce
2 cups ketchup
1 T. heaping, prepared
   mustard

Cut bacon in small pieces and fry until crisp. Remove bacon. Fry onions in bacon grease. Add all ingredients together including bacon grease and heat in slow cooker if desired or bake until heated through and bubbly.

Hungarian Noodles

3 chicken bouillon cubes
¼ cup boiling water
1 10¾-oz. can cream of
  mushroom soup
½ cup chopped onion
2 T. Worcestershire sauce
⅛–¼ tsp. hot pepper sauce

⅛–¼ tsp. garlic powder
2 cups cottage cheese
2 cups sour cream
1 lb. noodles, cooked and
  drained
¼ cup shredded Parmesan
  cheese
paprika

Dissolve bouillon in water. Add the next five ingredients; mix well. Stir in cottage cheese, sour cream, and noodles and mix well. Pour into greased 2½-quart casserole dish. Sprinkle with the Parmesan cheese and paprika. Cover and bake at 350° for 45 minutes or until heated through. (Casserole may be covered and refrigerated overnight. Allow to stand at room temperature for 30 minutes before baking.) Yield: 8–10 servings.

YEAST
BREADS

Sour Cream Twists

2 cups sour cream
¼ cup margarine
2 packages yeast (4½ tsp.),
  dissolved in ¼ c. warm
  water
6 T. sugar
2 eggs, beaten
½ tsp. baking soda
2 tsp. salt

6 cups flour
soft butter
brown sugar
cinnamon

Glaze:
2 cups powdered sugar
2 T. milk
1 tsp. vanilla

*The less a
thing can be
proved the
hotter we
get arguing
about it.*

Bring sour cream to a boil. Melt margarine in sour cream. Cool to lukewarm. Mix sour cream mixture, yeast mixture, sugar, eggs, soda, salt, and flour. Knead well. Let stand 15 minutes. Divide in half and roll out each half 9 inches wide. Spread with soft butter, brown sugar, and cinnamon. Fold over to 4½ inches wide. Cut into 1-inch strips. Twist each strip twice and put on a greased cookie sheet. Press ends to pan to seal and anchor. Let rise until double. Bake at 350° for 12 minutes. Glaze. Makes two cookie sheets full.

For glaze: Mix all ingredients until smooth. Add milk if not thin enough to drizzle. Drizzle onto twists.

Dilly Rolls

2 cups small curd cottage
    cheese
2 T. butter
2 packages (4½ tsp.) active
    dry yeast
½ cup warm water
2 eggs

¼ cup sugar
2 T. dried minced onion
1–2 T. dill weed
1 T. salt
½ tsp. baking soda
4½–5 cups flour

In a large saucepan, over medium heat, cook cottage cheese and butter until butter is melted. Cool to warm (not hot). In a large mixing bowl, dissolve yeast in water. Add eggs, sugar, onion, dill, salt, baking soda, and cottage cheese mixture. Add 3 cups flour; beat until smooth. Add enough remaining flour to form a soft dough. Turn onto a floured surface; knead until smooth and elastic, about 6–8 minutes. Place in a greased bowl, turning once to grease top. Cover and let rise in warm place until doubled, about 1 hour. Punch dough down. Form into 24 balls; place in a greased 13 x 9-inch baking pan. Cover and let rise until doubled, about 45 minutes. Bake at 350° for 20–25 minutes. You can also make these without the onion and dill if you want to.

Caramel-Pecan Monkey Bread

1 package (2¼ tsp.) active dry
    yeast
¼ cup warm water
1¼ cups warm milk
⅓ cup butter, melted
¼ cup sugar
2 eggs

1 tsp. salt
5 cups flour

Caramel:

⅔ cup brown sugar
¼ cup butter, cubed
¼ cup heavy whipping cream

Assembly:

¾ cup chopped pecans
1 cup sugar
1 tsp. cinnamon
½ cup butter, melted

In a large bowl, dissolve yeast in warm water. Add the milk, butter, sugar, eggs, salt, and 3 cups flour. Beat on medium speed for 3 minutes. Stir in enough remaining flour to form a firm dough. Turn onto floured surface; knead until smooth and elastic, about 6–8 minutes. Place in a greased bowl, turning once to grease the top. Cover and refrigerate overnight.

For caramel: In a small saucepan, bring the brown sugar, butter, and cream to a boil. Cook and stir for 3 minutes. Pour half into a greased 10-inch fluted pan; sprinkle with half of the pecans.

Assembly: Punch dough down; shape into 40 balls (each about 1¼ inches in diameter). In a shallow bowl, combine sugar and cinnamon. Place melted butter in another bowl. Dip balls in butter, and then roll in sugar mixture. Place 20 balls in the tube pan; top with remaining caramel and pecans. Top with remaining balls.

Cover and let rise until doubled, about 45 minutes. Bake at 350° for 30–35 minutes or until golden brown. (Cover loosely with foil if top browns too quickly.) Cool for 10 minutes before inverting onto a serving plate. Serve warm.

It is difficult to take advice from some people since they need it so badly themselves.

Mamm's Bread

2 T. yeast	2 T. salt
1 tsp. sugar	1 cup brown sugar
2 cups warm water	6 cups whole wheat flour
4 cups hot water	14 cups bread flour
⅔ cup oil	butter

Add yeast and 1 teaspoon sugar to warm water. Set aside. In a very large bowl, put hot water, oil, salt, and brown sugar. Stir to dissolve. Add 4 cups of the whole wheat flour; beat well. Add the last of the whole wheat flour and 2 cups bread flour and the yeast mixture and beat well. Gradually add the rest of the flour. When too hard to stir, turn onto floured surface and knead in the rest of the flour. Add or subtract flour for right consistency. It should be easy to handle when finished. Grease a large bowl; put dough in and turn so that top is greased. Cover and let rise 1 hour. Punch down. Let rise another hour. Shape into loaves; put into greased bread pans. Cover and let rise until doubled (1–2 hours). Do not preheat oven. Bake at 350° for 35–45 minutes, or until bread is done (makes a hollow sound when thumped). Remove from pans and butter tops. I just rub a stick of butter over the tops. Let cool. Makes 7–8 loaves.

Mamm's Refrigerator Dinner Rolls

½ cup warm water	1 T. salt
2 packages (4½ tsp.) yeast	⅓ cup shortening
1½ cups lukewarm milk	2 eggs
½ cup sugar	6¼–6¾ cups flour

Soak yeast in water 5 minutes. Combine milk, sugar, and salt. Stir to dissolve. Beat in shortening, eggs, yeast mixture, and 1 cup flour until smooth. Add remaining flour; stir until dough leaves sides of bowl. Turn onto floured surface; knead until smooth, elastic, and no longer sticky (5–10 minutes). Place in greased bowl, turning so top of dough is greased also. Cover with waxed paper and a damp cloth. Place in refrigerator. Punch down dough as it rises. Keep cloth damp. Dough will keep 3 days in refrigerator. Shape dough directly from refrigerator into desired shapes. Let rise until doubled, 1½ to 2 hours. Bake at 375° for 15–20 minutes. Makes 4 dozen.

Pizza Crust

1 cup warm water	2 T. oil
1 T. yeast	½ tsp. salt
1 tsp. sugar	3–3½ cups flour

Stir yeast and sugar into warm water. Let set a bit. Add the rest of the ingredients. Knead for a couple minutes. Let sit 5 minutes. Press into greased cookie sheet or pizza pan. Bake at 400° a few minutes. It should look dry but not browned. Add pizza sauce and toppings and bake about 15 minutes more.

Whole Wheat Bread

2 packages (4½ tsp.) active
    dry yeast
1 tsp. sugar
¾ cup warm water
2 cups lukewarm milk
    (scalded then cooled)

¼ cup honey
3 T. shortening
1 T. salt
7–8 cups whole wheat flour
butter

It is good to pick your friends, but not to pieces.

Dissolve yeast and sugar in warm water. Mix milk, honey, shortening, salt, and 4 cups of the flour. Add yeast mixture and 2 cups flour; beat until smooth. Add enough remaining flour to make dough easy to handle. Turn dough onto floured surface and knead until smooth and elastic, about 10 minutes. (Add more flour if necessary.) Place in greased bowl; turn greased side up. Cover; let rise in warm place until doubled, about 1 hour. (Dough is ready if indentation remains when touched.) Punch down dough; divide into halves. Roll each half into a rectangle, 18 x 9 inches. Fold 9-inch sides crosswise into thirds, overlapping ends. Roll up tightly, beginning at narrow end. Pinch edge of dough into roll to seal well; press in ends of roll. Press each end with side of hand to seal; fold ends under. Place loaves seam side down in two greased loaf pans. Cover and let rise in warm place till doubled, about 1 hour. Heat oven to 375°. Place loaves on lowest rack so that tops of loaves are in center of oven. Bake until loaves are deep golden brown and sound hollow when tapped, 30 to 35 minutes. Immediately remove from pans. Take a stick of butter and generously rub over the tops. Cool.

Variation: For white bread, substitute 3 tablespoons sugar for the honey and white flour for the whole wheat.

Freeze-and-Bake Knots

2 packages (4½ tsp.) yeast
1½ cups warm water
2 tsp. plus ½ cup sugar
   divided
1½ cups warm milk

¼ cup vegetable oil
4 tsp. salt
7½–8½ cups flour
melted butter

Dissolve yeast in warm water. Add 2 teaspoons sugar; let stand for 5 minutes. Add milk, oil, salt, remaining sugar, and 2 cups flour; beat until smooth. Stir in enough remaining flour to form stiff dough. Knead on floured surface until smooth and elastic, about 6–8 minutes. Place in a greased bowl, turning once to grease top. Cover and let rise in a warm place until doubled, about 1½ hours. Punch dough down. Turn onto lightly floured surface; divide into four pieces. Cover three pieces with plastic wrap. Divide remaining piece into 12 balls. To form knots, roll each ball into a 10-inch rope; tie into a knot and pinch ends together. Repeat with remaining dough. Place rolls on greased baking sheets; brush with butter. Cover and let rise until doubled, about 20–30 minutes. To serve immediately, bake at 375° for 15–18 minutes. To freeze for later use, partially bake at 300° for 15 minutes. Remove from pans to wire racks to cool; freeze. Reheat frozen rolls at 375° for 12–15 minutes or until browned.

Maple Oat Batter Bread

1¼ cups warm milk (120°–130°)

1 cup quick-cooking oats

¼ cup butter, softened

1 package (2¼ tsp.) yeast

¼ cup warm water

⅓ cup maple syrup

1½ tsp. salt

1 egg, lightly beaten

¾ cup whole wheat flour

2 cups flour

additional oats

Combine the milk, oats, and butter; cool to 110°–115°. Dissolve yeast in warm water; add to the oat mixture. Add the syrup, salt, egg, whole wheat flour, and 1 cup flour. Beat on low speed for 30 seconds; beat on high for 3 minutes. Stir in remaining flour (batter will be thick). Do not knead.

Sprinkle additional oats into a greased 1½-quart baking dish. Spoon batter into dish. Cover and let rise in warm place until doubled, about 50 minutes. Bake at 350° for 40–45 minutes or until golden brown. Cool for 10 minutes before removing from pan. Serve warm.

Rebecca's Vanilla Cinnamon Rolls

From *Rebecca's Return*

"Rebecca's home," ten-year-old Katie said, sticking her head into the kitchen. "Yummy—cinnamon rolls!" Tall for her age, she had black hair like Rebecca. Her sisters were right behind her.
"Hi, girls," Rebecca told them and glanced their way.

2 cups cold milk

1 3.4-oz. package instant vanilla pudding mix

2 packages (4½ tsp.) yeast

½ cup warm water

½ cup plus 2 T. butter, melted, divided

2 eggs

2 T. sugar	*Frosting:*
1 tsp. salt	1 cup brown sugar
6 cups flour	½ cup heavy whipping cream
½ cup brown sugar	½ cup butter, cubed
1 tsp. cinnamon	2 cups powdered sugar

Whisk together the milk and pudding for 2 minutes; set aside.
Dissolve yeast in warm water. Add ½ cup butter, eggs, sugar,
salt, and 2 cups flour. Beat on medium speed for 3 minutes.
Add pudding; beat until smooth. Stir in enough flour to form a
soft dough (dough will be sticky). Turn onto a floured surface;
knead until smooth and elastic, about 6–8 minutes. Place in a
greased bowl, turning once to grease top. Cover and let rise in
a warm place until doubled, about 1 hour. Punch dough down.
Turn onto floured surface; divide in half. Roll each portion into
an 18 x 11-inch rectangle; brush with remaining butter. Combine
brown sugar and cinnamon; sprinkle over dough to within ½
inch of edges. Roll up jelly-roll style, starting with long side;
pinch seams to seal. Cut each into 16 slices. Place cut side down
in two greased 13 x 9-inch pans. Cover and let rise until doubled,
about 30 minutes. Bake at 350° for 20–25 minutes or until
golden brown.

For frosting: Meanwhile, in saucepan, combine the brown sugar,
cream, and butter. Bring to a boil; cook and stir for 2 minutes.
Remove from the heat. Beat in the powdered sugar until creamy.
Frost rolls. Serve warm.

*People
with weak
arguments
have to
develop
strong
voices.*

Milk-and-Honey White Bread

2 packages (4½ tsp.) yeast	¼ cup butter, melted
2½ cups warm milk	2 tsp. salt
⅓ cup honey	8–8½ cups flour

Dissolve yeast in warm milk. Add the honey, butter, salt, and 5 cups flour; beat until smooth. Stir in enough remaining flour to form a soft dough. Turn onto a floured surface and knead until smooth and elastic (adding flour if necessary), 6–8 minutes. Place in a greased bowl, turning once to grease top. Cover and let rise until doubled, about 1 hour. Punch dough down. Divide in half; shape each portion into a loaf. Place in two greased loaf pans. Cover and let rise until doubled, about 30 minutes. Bake at 375° for 30–35 minutes or until golden brown (cover loosely with foil if top browns too quickly). Remove from pans to wire racks to cool.

Bread Sticks

1½ cups warm water	**Butter Mixture:**
1 T. yeast	½ cup butter, melted
1 T. oil	3 T. olive oil
1 T. sugar	3 T. Parmesan cheese
1 tsp. salt	1 tsp. garlic powder
4 cups flour	2–3 T. Italian seasoning
	extra Parmesan cheese

Dissolve yeast in warm water; add oil, sugar, and salt. Stir in flour until it is too stiff to stir with a spoon. Put onto a floured surface and knead several times. Let rise until doubled. Roll out on a floured surface 15 inches square. Cut dough into strips with a pizza cutter. Cut each strip into 3 pieces. Dip pieces into butter mixture and place on cookie sheet. Let rise for 20–30 minutes. Sprinkle with a bit of Parmesan cheese. Bake at 350° for 15–18 minutes or until golden. Delicious served with marinara sauce.

Homemade Brown Bread

1½ cups boiling water
1 cup old-fashioned oats
2 T. shortening
2 tsp. salt
1 package (2¼ tsp.) yeast
¾ cup warm water

½ tsp. sugar
¼ cup brown sugar
¼ cup molasses
4¾–5¼ cups flour
butter

Combine the first 4 ingredients. Cool to 110°–115°. In a mixing bowl, dissolve yeast in warm water. Sprinkle with sugar. Add oat mixture, brown sugar, molasses, and 3 cups flour; mix well. Add enough remaining flour to form a soft dough. Turn onto floured surface and knead until smooth and elastic, about 6–8 minutes. Place in a greased bowl; turn once to grease top. Cover and let rise in a warm place until doubled, about 1 hour. Punch dough down. Divide in half; shape into loaves. Place into two greased loaf pans. Cover and let rise until doubled, about 30–45 minutes. Bake at 350° for 30–35 minutes or until golden brown. Remove from pans; rub butter over tops. Cool.

Golden Crescents

2 packages (4½ tsp.) yeast
¾ cup warm water
½ cup sugar
¼ cup plus 2 T. butter,
    softened and divided
2 T. shortening

2 eggs
1 tsp. salt
4–4½ cups flour or bread
    flour
additional butter, melted

Dissolve yeast in water. Add sugar, ¼ cup butter, shortening, eggs, salt, and 2 cups flour; beat until smooth. Add enough of the remaining flour to form a soft dough. Turn onto a floured surface; knead until smooth and elastic, (adding flour if necessary) 6–8 minutes. Place in a greased bowl; turn once to grease top. Cover and let rise in a warm place until doubled, about 1½ hours. Punch the dough down; divide in half. Roll each half into a 12-inch circle. Brush remaining butter over dough. Cut each circle into 12 wedges. Roll up wedges from the wide end and curve to form a crescent. Place the point down 2 inches apart on greased cookie sheets. Cover and let rise until doubled, about 45 minutes. Bake at 375° for 8–10 minutes or until golden brown. Brush with butter if desired. Yield: 2 dozen.

Opportunities always look better going than coming.

Deacon's Light as a Feather Donuts

2 packages (4½ tsp.) yeast
1½ cups warm milk
1 cup cold mashed potatoes
1½ cups sugar, divided
½ cup vegetable oil
2 tsp. salt
2 tsp. vanilla

½ tsp. baking soda
½ tsp. baking powder
2 eggs
5½–6 cups flour
½ tsp. cinnamon
cooking oil for deep-fat frying

Dissolve yeast in warm milk. Add potatoes, ½ cup sugar, oil, salt, vanilla, soda, baking powder, and eggs; mix well. Add enough flour to form a soft dough. Place in a greased bowl, turning once to grease top. Cover and let rise in a warm place until doubled, about 1 hour. Punch dough down; roll out on a floured surface to ½-inch thickness. Cut with a 3-inch doughnut cutter. Place on greased baking sheets; cover and let rise until almost doubled, about 45 minutes. Meanwhile, combine the cinnamon and remaining sugar; set aside. Heat oil to 350°; fry donuts until golden on both sides. Drain on paper towels; roll in cinnamon-sugar while still warm.

Wholesome Wheat Bread

2 packages (4½ tsp.) yeast
2¼ cups warm water
3 T. sugar
⅓ cup butter
⅓ cup honey

½ cup instant nonfat dry milk powder
1 T. salt
4½ cups whole wheat flour
2¾–3½ cups flour or bread flour

Dissolve yeast in water. Add sugar, butter, honey, milk powder, salt, and whole wheat flour; beat until smooth. Add enough flour to form soft dough. Turn onto a floured surface; knead until smooth and elastic, about 10 minutes. Place in a greased bowl, turning once to grease top. Cover and let rise in a warm place until doubled, about 1 hour. Punch down. Shape dough into 2 traditional loaves. Place in greased loaf pans. Cover and let rise until doubled, about 30 minutes. Bake at 350° for 30–35 minutes. Remove from pans to wire racks.

Ruth's Donuts

1 package (2¼ tsp.) yeast
3 tsp. lukewarm water
2 tsp. sugar
½ cup shortening
½ cup sugar

1 T. salt
2 egg yolks
3½ cups lukewarm water
approximately 8¼ cups flour

Mix first 3 ingredients in small container; stir well. Let stand until dissolved. In a mixing bowl, combine shortening, ½ cup sugar, salt, and egg yolks. Add yeast mixture. Cream very well. Add 3½ cups lukewarm water. Stir to combine, then add flour a little at a time to make soft dough. Do not knead with hands. Cover and let rise until doubled in size. Punch down, then chill in refrigerator for 1½–2 hours. Roll out dough and cut out donuts. Cover with plastic wrap and let rise 1 additional hour, then deep-fat fry at 375°. This dough can be kept in the refrigerator for a week.

Glaze for Donuts

2 egg whites
2 lbs. powdered sugar

¾ cup hot water
1 tsp. vanilla

Beat egg whites lightly in bowl. Add powdered sugar, then pour hot water and vanilla over top. Beat until glaze is smooth but not foamy. Brush over cooled donuts.

Herbed Oatmeal Pan Bread

1½ cups boiling water
1 cup old-fashioned oats
2 packages (4½ tsp.) yeast
½ cup warm water
¼ cup sugar
3 T. butter, softened
2 tsp. salt
1 egg
4–4¾ cups flour

Topping:
¼ cup butter, melted, divided
2 T. grated Parmesan cheese
1 tsp. dried basil
½ tsp. dried oregano
½ tsp. garlic powder

Combine boiling water and oats; cool to 110–115 degrees. In a large mixing bowl, dissolve yeast in warm water. Add the sugar, butter, salt, egg, oat mixture, and 2 cups flour; beat until smooth. Stir in enough remaining flour to form a soft dough.

Turn onto a floured surface; knead until smooth and elastic, about 6–8 minutes. Place in a greased bowl, turning once to grease top. Cover and let rise in warm place until doubled, about 45 minutes.

Punch dough down. Press evenly into a greased 13 x 9-inch pan. With a very sharp knife, cut diagonal lines 1½ inches apart completely through dough. Repeat in opposite direction, creating diamond pattern. Cover and let rise until doubled, about 1 hour.

Redefine pattern by gently poking along cut lines with knife tip. Brush with 2 tablespoons melted butter. Bake at 375° for 15 minutes. Meanwhile, combine dry topping ingredients. Brush bread with remaining butter; sprinkle with cheese mixture. Bake for 5 minutes longer. Serve warm.

*The Amish man and his young son made
a visit into town, stopping in at the
high-rise hotel to look around. Inside
the lobby, they saw the row of elevators
with their blinking lights overhead.
Gawking, they watched people getting on
and off. Once the crowd had cleared, an
older lady approached the elevator and
disappeared inside. Moments later the
lights blinked again, and the door opened.
A much younger woman stepped out.
The Amish man turned to his son
and said, "Let's go home at once
and bring* Mamm *back here."*

INDEX

Jerry Eicher's bestselling Amish fiction (more than 400,000 in combined sales) includes The Adams County Trilogy, the Hannah's Heart books, The Fields of Home, and the Little Valley series. After a traditional Amish childhood, Jerry taught for two terms in Amish and Mennonite schools in Ohio and Illinois. Since then he's been involved in church renewal, preaching, and teaching Bible studies.

Tina Eicher was born and married in the Amish faith, surrounded by a mother and sisters who were great Amish cooks. At fellowship meals and family gatherings, Tina's dishes receive high praise and usually return empty.

Jerry and Tina are the parents of four children and live in Virginia.